What Do We Believe?
Why Does it Matter?

Other titles in the Learning Church Series

LEARNING CHURCH

What Do We Believe?
Why Does it Matter?

Jeff Astley

scm press

Published in 2016 by SCM Press
Editorial office
3rd Floor
Invicta House
108–114 Golden Lane
London
EC1Y 0TG

SCM Press is an imprint of Hymns Ancient & Modern Ltd
(a registered charity)
13A Hellesdon Park Road
Norwich NR6 5DR, UK

www.scmpress.co.uk

British Library Cataloguing in Publication data

A catalogue record for this book is available
from the British Library

978 0 334 05405 4

Typeset by Manila Typesetting
Printed and bound by
CPI Group (UK) Ltd, Croydon

Contents

Preface

This volume in the Learning Church series is for readers who are embarking for the first time on the study of Christian doctrine or of Christian theology more broadly, either as independent learners or as part of a programme of study in Christian discipleship or ministry. It is intended as a general introduction to the basic beliefs of Christianity, which also highlights something of their significance for Christian living, thinking and worship, as well as some of the intellectual difficulties to which these beliefs give rise.

We shall be exploring in this short book themes that lie at the heart of the Church's teachings, as they have been captured by the Church's creeds. The exploration will include sampling the variety of ways in which Christians – including the present author – have understood these credal claims. This is intended to help readers to engage – individually or as a group – in a 'conversation' with these different theological positions, and to encourage reflection on the strengths and weaknesses of their own beliefs as well as those of others. The ultimate aim of this book is not only to provide information but also to assist its readers to discern what matters *to them* about these beliefs – how Christian teachings *work* for them, spiritually, religiously and practically.

In writing this primer I will draw on my experience of teaching doctrine to a range of people in a wide variety of contexts and institutions, especially in Lincoln and Durham. I am grateful to the many undergraduate students, ordinands and other adult learners whose reflections on the relevance of Christian teaching to their lives have tested and encouraged my own. My thanks are also due to Evelyn Jackson for the trouble she has taken in typing the manuscript for this book.

Jeff Astley
November 2015

1

Christian Beliefs:
Diversity, Disputes and Meanings

Who cares what you believe? Well, obviously, *you* do.

To 'believe' something is to hold that it is *true*, to accept that it says something that is a *fact*, and that what it states or proposes or claims somehow corresponds to some part of reality. To believe is to think that this thing or event is – or was – *real*, and that statements about it are not mistakes or falsehoods, fictions or pretences (although, of course, they may be).

We believe lots of stuff that doesn't really matter all that much to us: that William the Conqueror won the battle of Hastings, that holly is an evergreen shrub, that Jupiter is 'a long way' from the earth (beliefs don't have to be very precise), that Richard III is buried in York Minster (he isn't, but beliefs are still beliefs – things we accept as true – even when they are false). *Religious* beliefs are different because they *involve us*. In this way they resemble some other beliefs, in particular beliefs about people to whom we are close and beliefs about how we ought to behave and the sort of values we should hold. Beliefs like these matter to us.

To believe that this universe is God's creation, or that Jesus is God's Messiah is, for Christians, part of the orientation of their lives. It is part of what gives it meaning for them – for us. We don't just believe *that* these claims are true; we commit ourselves to them, trust in them, often rejoice in them, and always rest our hearts – and not only our minds – in them. We say, therefore, that we 'believe *in*' these realities, as well as holding beliefs *about* them. And we do this with varying degrees of passion. Passion is usually a good measure of what it is that we *really* believe in, and of what truly concerns us.

Elsewhere in this series I have written about the *form* of belief and its relationship to experience, practice and, especially, faith (Astley, 2014, esp. Ch. 4). In this new book, however, our concern is not so much with *how* we believe but with *what* we believe: with the *content* of our believing and of 'the Christian faith'.

Coming out of hiding

We are not always fully aware of our beliefs; some of them are implicit rather than explicit. You have probably more than once had the strange experience of becoming aware of what you actually believe about something or especially about someone. It is not always a pleasant realization.

And it is the same with our religious beliefs. 'Ordinary theology' is my name for the reflective but rather unsystematic and un-argued religious beliefs that most of us have and hold before we ever study any sort of academic theology. These beliefs mainly stay with us afterwards, however modified they may become by more scholarly arguments and understandings, and they continue to constitute the personal and powerful core of our own developing theology (see Astley, 2014, Chs 1 and 2; Astley and Christie, 2007). Those who research these beliefs through the medium of interviews are used to hearing Christians, whether life-long churchgoers or new converts, confessing that talking about their faith 'has helped me understand what it is that I really believe', or even that 'I hadn't realized before that this is what I believe'. This is not because their beliefs had been repressed or consciously hidden but because many of our beliefs are often located in the shadows and hollows of our minds and hearts, and the chaos of our living, rather than lying out there in plain sight where they can be clearly illuminated and deliberately ordered. Studying doctrine is also a way of bringing our more implicit religious beliefs 'out of hiding', as we respond to reading about other people's beliefs by asking, 'What do *I* believe about it?' And by adding, very often, 'Well, I certainly don't believe *that*', with reference to some venerable piece of doctrine – or perhaps Jeff Astley's more recent, less impressive and more confused theology.

TO DO

Before reading further, please attempt to write down (your interpretation of) the set of Christian beliefs *that matter most to you*. Why are they so significant for you?

What Christian beliefs have you left out, and why?

Diversity and disputes

In the end, we can only believe what *we* can believe. And in religion it matters to us what we believe. No amount of hearing or saying – or even singing – the Nicene Creed, at whatever volume, will erase our beliefs and replace them with the agreed formulations of the Church. What actually happens when we learn about what other Christians believe, or when we think about what the Church holds that we ought to believe as Christians, is that our believing enters into some sort of dialogue or 'conversation', which is itself often implicit and may even be unconscious, in which the Church speaks but so do we. In this process the two sets of ideas interact, with the result that our own beliefs shift and sharpen, are qualified or are overturned, as they are either challenged or endorsed.

But there will be no real change in our believing unless the creeds 'speak to us' at the level of our hearts, addressing what matters to us but doing so in a way that does not ignore the intellectual difficulties posed by our heads (cf. Astley, 2014, Ch. 3).

We should not be surprised, therefore, that both the background and foreground of the Church's creeds are marked by argument and dispute. Agreement was sometimes hard won in their formulation, as *orthodoxy* ('right opinion') was defined over against the other 'choices' that became viewed as *heresy*. Church politics and rivalry had their part to play in this, but the creeds 'were also the fruit of devoted study, reflection and prayer' (Wiles, 1999, p. 28).

That is their background. But the creeds have a foreground too, represented by the history that lies between their creation in the early centuries of Christianity and our inheriting them in our own day. This period constitutes a long debate over the different inter-pretations and degrees of credence that have been applied to these doctrines. This debate was also the result of devotion, study and prayer, as well as the product of new intellectual doubts and differ-ent ways of thinking.

Christian doctrine as we now receive it is therefore diverse. There are different ways in which Christian truth has been understood, and doctrinal disagreements continue today between and within different schools of theological expression, as well as the vari-ous denominations and congregations that make up the present Christian Church. As this doctrinal diversity is not likely to go away any time soon, we had better get used to it.

My main point, however, is this: if any doctrine is to become and be (in whatever way) *your* doctrine, your belief, it must have a mean-ing for you that makes sense – a meaning by which you can think, but also worship, pray and live. In this respect, doctrine must 'work for you'. And in order to manage that, it must have some sort of fit with your understanding of and feelings about life, the universe and everything, and especially your beliefs about God.

Your view of God will have originated from a variety of sources and not just from the creeds. It came from your reading and hear-ing of, and reflections on, the Christian Scriptures and the Christian 'tradition' (the teaching and practice of the Church), insofar as you regard these things as revealing God's nature, character, relation-ships and actions. It will also have been shaped by your own experi-ences of both life and the life of faith. And it will now be understood through the 'critical' (that is, reflective and evaluative) lens of your reason and understanding, and filtered through the context of a shared, contemporary culture and its language – for 'if theology is to be intelligible, it has to use the language of the culture within which it is undertaken' (Macquarrie, 1977, p. 13). We can only understand what *we* can understand.

As you reflect on the doctrines of the creeds, you are part of the conversation that constitutes all Christian teaching and Christian learning (cf. Astley, 2010, pp. 9–20).

> God is complicated, which means doctrine is also. We need stu-
> dents of theology to continue to challenge the 'received' answers.
> But we do so on the assumption that there are better and worse
> ways of making sense of God. We are on the quest for the truth;
> and our arguments are often a valuable way of discovering that
> truth. (Markham, 2008, p. 2)

(And 'our arguments' include 'yours', of course . . .)

The use of Scripture

This book will encourage you to read a good number of passages from the Bible, as part of our exploration of Christian doctrine. I should explain right away that these are not to be regarded in any sense as 'proof texts'.[1] Instead, we should normally treat scriptural texts as first steps – or general direction pointers – towards a doctrinal theme and how it may be formulated. They also serve as illustrative material of, or challenges to, a particular doctrine; and as suggestions for alternative paths that you may wish to follow in your own reflections on what Christians do and should believe.

There is no short and easy path – no quick direct route – between the Bible and Christian doctrine. Even the most emphatically 'Bible-based'

---

1 A proof text is an isolated, out-of-context, biblical quotation that is employed to 'prove a point'. Dangers in this practice include the risk of selecting such texts in a way that is unrepresentative, and employing a text in a way that does not accurately reflect its original use or a text whose source as a whole may not actually support the argument we are seeking to advance.

theology views the Scriptures through its own theological spectacles, so its doctrines are never just 'read off' Scripture. A further issue is that biblical and doctrinal language often operate in different ways and fulfil different functions. To return to the original metaphor, however, it is crucially important that these two ends of the journey of Christian thinking, the biblical and the doctrinal, should be connected, and that this connection should never be broken. (For more on these issues, see pp. 44–8.)

The doctrinal journey

In such a short book we shall have to be quite selective about the Christian beliefs that we explore. The creeds have led the way in this, particularly the shorter (so-called) Apostles' Creed, which is a creed that is common to the Roman Catholic and Protestant Churches of 'Western Christianity'. The chapters that follow will reflect the main concerns both of this creed and of the more universal Nicene Creed, while adding something about some of the major doctrines and problems of belief that they only hint at, such as justification, atonement, the philosophy of God and the problem of evil.

This volume will diverge from the order of the creeds, however, because – as I shall contend in Chapter 2 – it is best to begin the doctrinal journey with our more concrete experiences of the Church, and those more personal and spiritual experiences of acceptance, healing and liberation whose implications are subsumed under the (contentious) doctrine of 'salvation'. So we shall begin our travels there, traversing these close and familiar trails before ascending gradually through the doctrines of the person and work of Christ, and then on to explore the distant terrain of the more abstract beliefs that concern God's mysterious nature and our ultimate destiny.

It might be useful at this point to remind ourselves of the content of these two creeds, from a modern translation (*English Language Liturgical Consultation* ©ELLC 1988).

Nicene Creed

We believe in one God,
the Father, the Almighty,
maker of heaven and earth,
of all that is,
seen and unseen.

We believe in one Lord, Jesus
    Christ,
the only Son of God,
eternally begotten of the Father,
God from God, Light from Light,
true God from true God,
begotten, not made,
of one Being with the Father;
through him all things were
    made.
For us and for our salvation he
    came down from heaven,
was incarnate from the Holy
    Spirit and the Virgin Mary
and was made man.
For our sake he was crucified
    under Pontius Pilate;
he suffered death and was
    buried.
On the third day he rose again
in accordance with the
    Scriptures;
he ascended into heaven
and is seated at the right hand
    of the Father.

Apostles' Creed

I believe in God, the Father
    almighty,
creator of heaven and earth.

I believe in Jesus Christ, his only
    Son, our Lord,
who was conceived by the Holy
    Spirit,
born of the Virgin Mary,
suffered under Pontius Pilate,
was crucified, died, and was
    buried;
he descended to the dead.
On the third day he rose again;
he ascended into heaven,
he is seated at the right hand of
    the Father,
and he will come to judge the
    living and the dead.

He will come again in glory to
   judge the living and the dead,
and his kingdom will have no
   end.

We believe in the Holy Spirit,
the Lord, the giver of life,
who proceeds from the Father
   and the Son,
who with the Father and
   the Son is worshipped and
   glorified,
who has spoken through the
   prophets.
We believe in one holy catholic
   and apostolic Church.
We acknowledge one baptism for
   the forgiveness of sins.
We look for the resurrection of
   the dead,
and the life of the world to come.
Amen.

I believe in the Holy Spirit,
the holy catholic Church,
the communion of saints,
the forgiveness of sins,
the resurrection of the body,
and the life everlasting.
Amen.

TO DO

Which parts of these creeds embody the most important elements
of *your own* Christian belief, and which parts are least significant for you?

Which passages in these creeds do you find difficult (a) to understand
and (b) to accept?

We should recognize, however, that these creeds are 'not "Articles
of Belief" or a system of doctrine, but rather "confessions" summarizing
the Christian story . . . They tell who God is and what he has done.

They invite the convert to make that story and that affirmation his or her own: the word for "confess" means also "acknowledge" and even "praise"' (Young, 2002, p. 12). In fact the creeds began life in the third century as synopses of faith used by baptismal candidates, having evolved from earlier sets of questions asked of them about their beliefs, to which the response was 'I believe' (Latin, *credo*). It was only later that the creeds became tests of orthodoxy, functioning as a court of appeal through their summing up of the common 'Rule of Faith', or standard of Christian truth. But this only strengthened their place as an integral – if on occasions disruptive – part of the Church's worship.

Faith has its home in prayer and worship, and in living and loving. This is where it often begins and to which it must return. The Christian faith and our faith as Christians are both expressed in Christian worship and Christian life. And Christian doctrines are deepened and enlarged as they are earthed in prayer, celebrated in worship and lived out in our relationships, work and play.

This link between doctrine and worship has always been particularly key. Worship is the place for praise, adoration, thanksgiving and confession, and for expressing the world's needs and our own. When we reflect on our faith – that is, when we do theology (which is often called 'faith seeking understanding') – we usually rise from our knees and step outside the context of worship. But we must never step too far away, or our theology will risk becoming arid and attenuated, losing both its passion and its point.

Good doctrine, therefore, should both arise out of and bring us back home to prayer. And it should arise out of and return us to life, also. *But it is no substitute for either.*

Following, learning, arguing

We can step away from worship but we can never walk away from life. The Christian faith is to be worked out and expressed, and so 'lived', in life – more concretely in *lives*, in *our* 'Christian lives'. So reflection on Christian doctrine can never be a purely theoretical or intellectual process – 'academic' in the bad sense of the term, as having no practical relevance. Hard thinking about God, even about theological 'theories', must connect at some level with how we live our lives. Otherwise it will cease to matter to us.

Charles Cranfield subtitled his slim book on the Apostles' Creed, 'A Faith to Live By'. He writes there that the creed 'must be studied and pondered . . . neither accepted nor rejected uncritically and without careful thought'. But he adds that 'we will certainly not have understood it if we fail to see its relevance to the life of the modern world, and to all the problems which that world presents' (Cranfield, 2004, p. 7). In learning about God we learn something about life, and in learning to live we may learn more about God. In both exercises, in truth, we may be said to 'learn God'. In the words of another Durham scholar, 'A person can be said to know God only if that person's whole life is being drawn into conformity to God . . . [As] one learns to love, as one learns justice, one is learning the nature of God' (Higton, 2008, p. 46).

But we shouldn't get too pious about this. Most theology is really done through hard thinking, discussing and arguing. Jesus' disciples argued on the road, and that led to a new, revised, deeper learning of Christ on their part (e.g. Mark 9.33–37; Luke 9.46–48). Theologians argue too; and so will you. But not as enemies. And not about everything. 'Studies of Christian doctrine mostly focus on points that are disputed and sometimes the impression is given that Christians disagree on everything. That is not true' (Lane, 2013, p. 6). This is fair enough. Still, we'd better expect *some* arguing on this journey.

Christian discipleship . . . is the practice of following Christ. A person learns how to follow Christ; in learning how to be a disciple one learns who Christ is. To be a disciple is to learn how to have faith in God by following Christ. Discipleship involves, indeed *is*, a way of life . . .

The rules guiding the practice are formulated in various ways. Most generally, the creeds incorporate the rule of the faith – but disciples seem to argue incessantly about how to form and follow those rules. The goal of the practice is, in its broadest sense, salvation – a life accepted as from God through Christ to be even now eternally enjoyed in the Spirit – though how we ought to formulate our understanding of that goal is one of the items about which we argue. Nonetheless, as one engaged in the practice one simultaneously learns how to be a disciple, that is, one who has the two-way relationship of 'having faith in' and 'being saved by' Christ. (Tilley, 2008, pp. 14–15)

TO DO

In what ways should the beliefs expressed in the creeds affect our Christian worship and Christian living?

Which parts of the creeds do you, and others you know, find most difficult to 'connect with' in these ways?

Further reading

Astley, J., 2010, *SCM Studyguide to Christian Doctrine*, London: SCM Press, Chs 1 and 2.

Burnaby, J., 1959, *The Belief of Christendom: A Commentary on the Nicene Creed*, London: SPCK, pp. 1–18.

Higton, M., 2008, *SCM Core Text: Christian Doctrine*, London: SCM Press, Ch. 1.

McGrath, A. E., 2008, *Theology: The Basics*, Oxford: Blackwell, pp. xiii–xxviii.

Pannenberg, W., 1972, *The Apostles' Creed in the Light of Today's Questions*, London: SCM Press, pp. 1–14.

Young, F. M., 2002, *The Making of the Creeds*, London: SPCK, Ch. 1.

2

Church:
Holy but Inclusive, Varied
though United?

Why begin with the Church? There must be more instructive and attractive ways into Christian doctrine. Surely Christianity is first and foremost to do with Christ: it is a matter of following Jesus and responding to his life and teaching, death and resurrection – and to the story of God's encounter with men and women in which Jesus is the key character and the central, compelling focus. Or we might argue that Christianity is mainly about God, as Jesus' story was mainly about God, and the world's story also. Shouldn't we begin there, beginning at the beginning, as it were?

Well, of course, we could, and most text books on doctrine do broadly follow the order of the creeds: God (the Father Creator), Jesus (God's Son), the Holy Spirit, the Church, forgiveness of sins (plus baptism in the Nicene Creed) and our resurrection. But I think there is much to be said for following a path that leads from concrete to abstract and from the familiar and obvious to what is mysterious and transcendent (see pp. 110–11), and therefore more puzzling. This route also takes us from our present reality through to our future hope. The order adopted by the creeds might appear to be more 'logical' than this, but although Christian doctrines interconnect, we shouldn't think they simply flow deductively from one to another, from theology about God down to the theology of the 'life of the world to come'. The credal order represents, rather, an order of importance (God first, the Church and ourselves last), and a sort of temporal sequence too (God – then creation – Jesus – the Spirit in the Church – and last of all ourselves and our end).

It is an ancient maxim in theology, however, that although in the 'order of being' God is primary, as the ground of our existence, God doesn't come first in our own 'order of knowing' – the order in which we come to know about reality. From our human perspective, finite objects that we know through our senses come 'before' and stand 'in front of' God. And it is undeniable that the stretched forms of language – the 'analogies' – that we apply to God, such as 'wise' or 'good', are words we learnt first in their application to humans. Yet 'in the "order of being" . . . God always comes first, creating the world (and human beings in particular) in his likeness. . . . [So] these words apply primarily and more properly to God, and only secondarily to us' (Astley, 2004, p. 58). The same point may be made of the use of religious metaphors such as 'Father', which is a word we learnt to use in reference to human beings before we ever met it in the Bible, although it may also be claimed that God was a father before anyone else and that God's character and love reveal the true meaning of the word.

Theological learning begins where we are. And for Christians, and even for outsiders, the Church is very much in-your-face – or at least round the corner – as the concrete, visible-audible-tangible, present reality of Christianity, however inadequate and embarrassing it often turns out to be.

How is it for you?

I also think that, as a general rule, it is best to reflect on what *we* believe before studying the Church's teachings (Latin *doctrina*, from which our English word 'doctrine' comes). Hence the first exercise in this book. Engaging with the task in this order makes it more likely that we shall consciously address any tensions between the two. Wherever we begin, however, we need to ensure we do not follow any set of beliefs in an unreflective way. After all, a grown-up 'learning Church' should also be a self-reflective, self-critical 'thinking Church'.

These ways of proceeding are particularly important when we study the Church's beliefs about itself.

TO DO

From your own experience (whether you attend a church regularly or not), how would you describe the Church? Jot down the words or phrases that best represent how it appears to you.

One problem that this exercise raises is that of identifying *the extent of the Church*. Does the word best label a local church (for which it is helpful to use a lower case 'c'); that is, a congregation or body of Christians that usually gathers for worship in a parish church, chapel or cathedral? This is the concrete, visible community where we meet a small part of the whole Church (upper case 'C'), which is the worldwide Christian community, stretching across denominations, cultures and political boundaries. And even that wide grouping is often said to be no more than part of our Church, the part that is 'militant' (engaged in the spiritual warfare of fighting against evil) 'here in earth'. There is a still greater whole that includes the 'Church triumphant in heaven' (or paradise), and also – for some Christians – the Church 'expectant' (or 'penitent') in purgatory (see Chapter 9).

When the Apostles' Creed expresses our belief in '*the communion of saints*', this is usually taken to refer to fellowship with all Christians alive today – just as Paul applied the word 'saints' to all Christians – *and* to those Christians who walked before us in God's way towards their fulfilment in God (again, all of them, and not just the particularly devout or super-good, whom we tend to think of today when we hear the word 'saintly'). For some, the phrase also came to imply participation in the sacraments, the *sancta* (see Chapter 3).

Nonetheless, how we think of the whole Church will inevitably be affected by what we see of the local, smaller church that we attend (or, in some cases, stay away from). So before proceeding further, please attempt this additional exercise.

TO DO

Review your list of words and phrases that best capture your experience of the C/church and ask yourself whether some of them apply more accurately – or *only* apply – to your local church, or to one or other of these bigger ideas of Church.

What words and phrases express how you would wish the Church (on earth) to be. How else might you describe this *ideal Church*?

Discipleship and belonging

The quotation at the end of the last chapter located the creeds in the context of the practice of Christian discipleship. The Christian Churches – that is, denominations – have over recent years redis-covered the idea of Church as a 'community of disciples' (Dulles, 2002, Ch. XIII) and even as a group of 'missionary disciples' (Pope Francis, 2013, §§ 24, 40, 120, 173). As a consequence, many adult (lay) Christian education programmes are often described as 'disci-pleship courses' that offer 'education for discipleship' or 'developing discipleship'. And the full title of this series picks up this usage.

In the Gospels and the Acts of the Apostles, the Greek word *mathētēs*, 'disciple', occurs over 260 times. It means a learner, and is applied to the followers of Jesus, those who followed in his way – literally and/or metaphorically. Outside the New Testament the word was also applied to an *apprentice*. An apprentice was – and still is – someone for whom learning wasn't just a matter of acquiring teach-ing at an intellectual level but involved their being formed by their master in a range of other aspects, such as specific skills, behaviour, values and character virtues. In a similar manner Jesus was the master of the first disciples, 'not so much as a teacher of right doctrine, but rather as the master-craftsman whom they were to follow and imitate . . . [in their] apprenticeship to the work of the Kingdom' (Manson, 1963, p. 240; cf. Astley, 2007, Ch. 1). Although the word 'disciple' is absent from the vocabulary of the New Testament letters and later Christian texts, much of its meaning carried over into the idea of baptism, which was the universal gateway into the Church.

Many contemporary Christians resist the language of discipleship because they think of the first disciples as being special and as having been specially called, in ways that they are not (cf. Walton, 2013, p. 179). But we should remember that:

- 'there seems to have been no real distinction in Jesus' ministry between those who literally followed him and a much wider circle of discipleship which he also recognized' – including those who had not formally declared for him (Dunn, 1992, pp. 108–10, cf. 113 and Mark 9.38–40);
- 'the discipleship to which Jesus called was a discipleship for sinners' (Dunn, 1992, p. 91, cf. 70–2).

We may therefore reason that all Christians today are worthy to be called disciples provided that, in some manner and to some degree, they may be said to follow and to learn from Jesus.

But are they – are we – a *community* of disciples? And are we *saints*?

Symbolic Church

Symbols are things – and their representations in human language, action and art – that 'stand for' something else. The riot of metaphors that we find in Scripture, hymns and prayers vividly suggest to our imaginations different aspects, understandings or dimensions of Christ's multidimensional Church.

TO DO

Try to find examples to illustrate the following images and metaphors for the Church. Look first in the New Testament (Ephesians is a rich source) and your church's hymn or song book; but also, if possible, at liturgies (forms of public worship) and prayers, or religious art and sculpture. If they are available to you, a concordance (in print or online), together with an Internet search engine, will greatly assist in this task.

- Ark
- Building
- Body of Christ
- Bride of Christ
- Family
- People of God
- Sheep
- Vine

Can you think of others?
Which are your own preferred symbols of the Church, and why?

Marking the Church

The classical four 'marks' or 'notes' of the Church derive from the Nicene Creed, where it is designated 'one holy catholic and apostolic' (the Apostles' Creed has only 'the holy catholic' Church). Any cursory examination of the present Church, however, will confirm that this is how it should ideally be, how God intends it to be, rather than how it actually is now as a reality that we can observe. There is a difference – which is why it can be said that 'any Christian who does not love and hate the church simultaneously probably doesn't know the church very well' (Inbody, 2005, p. 251).

When the Church recites these clauses of its creeds, we must therefore think of it as committing itself to striving to *become* what it already *is* – but only is in God's intention and as our hope and aspiration.

One

Patently, the Church is not united. Nevertheless, the one God of all calls it to be one (John 17.11, 20–22). And the Church's one body, hope, faith and baptism (Ephesians 4.4–6) confirms this claim to unity, as expressed in God's desire. The implications of this claim and this call need to be felt closer to home than is suggested by the abstract aim of world ecumenism, which is something that is today often expressed only half-heartedly once a year, in the Week of Prayer for Christian Unity. But the Church's unity cannot wait upon organizational union or even intercommunion.

The idea of *community* is in essence the idea of people belonging together. It suggests a measure of equality in that belonging, in 'one communion and fellowship'. The English word 'Church' may be traced back to the Greek *kyriakon*, a term that means 'the Lord's belonging'. For Christians, belonging to one another is something that should naturally follow from belonging to, and following, one and the same Lord. It has been suggested that, as an inclusive 'beLonging' community, the Church has been placed in the world:

> to express the longing of God. . . . The Church is the first fruit of God's longing. Its life together, therefore, does not depend on excluding people and groups, but on a witness to the constantly inclusive activity of a God whose concern extends [to all]. (Selby, 1991, pp. 2–3)

Among all the metaphors for the Church in the Bible, the image of *the body of Christ* is the one that seems most relevant in this context. In some of the New Testament letters, Christ is the head of this body; but the main point of Paul's use of the image is that the body itself is a coordinated unity that can only function because of its diversity. In biology this is sometimes expressed as the 'differentiation and division of labour' that results from the growth and development of a complex organism or social grouping (e.g. of social insects like bees). It is essential to their lives.

TO DO

Read 1 Corinthians 12.12–30, in which Paul articulates this metaphor in detail. What are (a) the strengths and (b) the weaknesses of this image of the Church?

When you think about it, this is a very bold – even arrogant sounding – metaphor. It suggests that however lowly a 'member' of the Church we may feel ourselves to be, we are still honoured as part of – as constituting – not just the 'body of Christians' but *Christ's* body on earth. If we are, as Paul claims that we are, 'in Christ' (e.g. 2 Corinthians 2.17; 5.17; Galatians 3.27), and if we are filled with, and formed and guided by the Spirit of Christ (Romans 8.9; Galatians 5.18, 22–26), then our actions may be said to be his actions, and our words his words. And that is an astonishingly high claim to make. Is that how the Church looks to others, or even to ourselves? Of course, it is an ideal . . .

As Christ's body we are also called to be one integrated person. We might argue, then, not only that *diversity-in-unity* within the Church is possible but that it is also essential – or even that it is inevitable. We *must* be many and different, if we are truly to be one.

But does this mean we cannot be Christians on our own? Rowan Williams writes that the slogan of the Church's life is '"not without the other"; no I without a you, no I without a we' (Williams, 2007, p. 106). But if we *were* to be one, what might this mean for *individualism*? Does individualism have 'no place in Christianity', as another Archbishop of Canterbury, Michael Ramsey, argued (Ramsey, 1936, p. 38). Yet the Church must not squash people's individual character, the 'individuality' of (other) Christians (see Astley, 2010, pp. 88–90, 92–3). In this respect, some sort of balance must surely be struck between the many and the one.

Holy

We should be one, and we should also be saints – in New Testament Greek, *hoi hagioi*, 'the holy ones'. Really?

Holiness, like the Church's unity and its other marks, primarily exists in God's intention. Its actual existence depends on the working of God's grace – that is, God's forgiving love and empowerment – which is freely offered and given, despite our unworthiness. But it also depends on our behaviour, in response to and in cooperation with that grace. With these provisos, yes, the Church 'is' holy. Israel too was called to holiness (Leviticus 19.2: 'You shall be holy, for I the LORD your God am holy'), as were the first disciples (Matthew 5.48: 'Be perfect, therefore, as your heavenly Father is perfect').

But doesn't this take imitation several steps too far, attempting the impossible and trying to copy the character of God? (No wonder, then, that the Church fails this test.) According to some scholars, however, in Matthew's Gospel 'perfect' is a wider term than moral flawlessness and is used for 'spiritual maturity', and even being 'fully developed' (Borg, 2006, pp. 324–5; France, 2007, pp. 228–9). And 'as the context makes clear . . . "Be perfect" means to demonstrate a complete love . . . that expresses itself toward enemies as well as toward family and friends' (Evans, 2012, p. 136). We may also note that 'holiness' is a word that is related to 'wholeness'. So it could be argued that the word represents not 'a closed-off holiness of separation from the world, but a holiness or wholeness of embrace – a type of love' (Astley, 2010, p. 99). As Karl Barth expresses this, the Church as Christ's community 'points beyond itself. . . . In its deepest and most proper tendency it is not churchly, but worldly.' Such a Church must have open doors, for 'it is holy in its openness to the street, and even the alley, in its turning to the profanity of all human life' (Barth, 1956, p. 725). 'Christianity is not "sacred" . . . it is an out-and-out "worldly" thing open to all humanity' (Barth, 1966, p. 147). Further, the Church's holiness is always the holiness *of sinners*.

The Church's holy ones may be chosen and, in this sense, 'set apart'. This is a matter of being 'consecrated' or 'made sacred', but these ideas also constitute the root meaning of 'sacrifice'. 'The holiness of the church cannot mean separation from the world; for the God of the Bible is holy in his love . . . The holiness of the church is also fulfilled in Christian love' (Pannenberg, 1972, p. 156). And therefore 'this separation is not for privilege but for service' (Burnaby, 1959, p. 140).

Put like this, the Church's proud declaration of holiness becomes a humbling responsibility and a radical commitment to serve.

Catholic

Anglicans and other Protestants may be puzzled at being expected to affirm in their creeds that the Church is 'catholic'. But this term does not label a denomination (the 'Roman Catholic' Church). Its connotations, rather, are 'all-embracing' or 'universal'. A better word for this ideal is *worldwide*; a more challenging one might be *inclusive*.

The inclusiveness of the Church flows from its unity-in-diversity and its holiness-as-openness. Many, very different parts of the Church have from time to time proclaimed themselves as the 'one, true' Church, warning the rest of the world that it should beware all imitations. A true spirit of catholicity, however, must reject such divisive language. As catholic, the Church should cast aside any sectarianism and any prejudice and discrimination based on race, on social and economic class or national divisions, or on sex and gender. Many would say that the Church should also renounce divisions over other categories, and there has been much contention in recent years over the category of sexuality. These debates will no doubt continue, but what is indisputable is that an orientation and stance of acceptance and openness should be – as people say – 'part of the Church's DNA'. We might also understand it as an implication of Jesus' command to 'make disciples of *all* nations' (Matthew 28.19).

> ## TO DO
>
> In what ways do you think that (a) the whole Church and (b) your local church is more inclusive than society in general? And in what ways are they more exclusive?
>
> Can any of this exclusivity be defended, and if so on what grounds?

The catholicity of the Church is not just a function of geography. The term is also often used as a measure of its doctrinal orthodoxy. This understanding overlaps with the next mark of the Church, its 'apostolicity'.

Apostolic

If the Church's catholicity denotes its inclusive universal spread (in space, we might say), its apostolic credentials depend on its historical identity, or its continuity down time and through history.

We should note that 'identity' (being the same thing) and 'continuity' (continuing as the same thing) are often compatible with a considerable amount of change, and thus of divergence and diversity. This is true of each one of us. Your mind, body and character will have changed very much over your lifetime, for good or ill; but it is still you who have changed – these changes happen to *you*. In this sense 'you remain the same' person: from the baby photographed naked on the hearthrug (that hearthrug will date you, anyway); through those proud days showing off your new school uniform, and your embarrassed moments of early adolescence; right up until . . . Well, we should stop there, perhaps, as it can be so depressing for some of us to complete the sequence. My point is only that this is still 'the same you' despite a great deal of change. Similarly, we may affirm that it is the same Church despite all its changes.

But perhaps this claim about the Church is rather narrower than that. For the Church believes itself to be apostolic insofar as it continues the same basic teaching and practice of the apostles, who are traditionally regarded as the eyewitnesses and first guardians of its message. The Church's sameness of doctrine and activity, however, are features that are obviously open to challenge.

This credal affirmation has also been interpreted as the Church's call to continue the *mission* of the Church, its 'sending out' by God into the world to preach God's (same) word to, and express God's (same) love and service for God's changing world. ('Mission' comes from the Latin verb *mittere*, 'to send'; 'apostle' from the Greek verb *apostellein*, 'to send forth'.) Notice that God's mission – God's sending out – is more than evangelism; it was, and is, expressed in action as well. As our discipleship should also be. The liberation theologian Gustavo Gutiérrez writes, 'our discipleship is our appropriation of [Jesus'] message of life, his love of the poor, his denunciation of injustice, his sharing of bread, his hope of resurrection' (Gutiérrez, 1983, p. 96).

Clearly, if the Church is envisaged less as an institution and more as a *movement* (which is how it began, of course), then sent-outness – to coin a word – may be said to mark its direction of travel or its orientation to the world (towards the 'outsider'), whatever it continues to believe or practise. Yet if the idea of a Church and of being a Christian is to have any determinate meaning, and their identity any sort of integrity, there must be some limits to the Church's beliefs and practices. But what are these limits? What counts as being Christian and what doesn't? What kinds of believing, belonging and behaving go beyond the limits? *Liberal* Christians (and theologians) set these defining limits more widely – more 'freely' – than do more *conservative* Churches, churchgoers and theologians, whose first instinct is to 'conserve' the traditional teaching and practice of Christianity (see Astley, 2010, pp. 15–18). But each group has its boundaries, and those whose beliefs or practices lie beyond such boundaries will not be counted as being 'Church' or as being 'Christian'.

TO DO

Can you think of examples of belief and behaviour that, in your view, are incompatible with membership of the Church?

What action, if any, should the Church take to protect its identity against these 'deviations'?

Can you think of any examples of issues of identity in the history of the Church? How were they resolved – and how could they have been resolved better?

Roman Catholics and others sometimes speak of associations of individuals, and frequently of the whole of the laity, as being an *'apostolate'*; that is, people who are responsible for the dissemination of the faith and of Christian salvation through their witness, love and social action, in whatever location they have been placed by God. This is an apt word for expressing the Church's perpetuation and extension of the apostles' mission, and for reminding us where the responsibility, privilege and power for this work truly lies.

Church of God or kingdom of heaven?

The Nicene Creed affirms that Christ's 'kingdom will have no end'. The kingdom of God (= 'kingdom of heaven' in Matthew's Gospel) is not a place, except metaphorically. In the New Testament it refers to the society in which God rules as king, where his will is being established 'on earth as it is in heaven'. It is inaugurated by and therefore present in Jesus' coming, ministry and teaching, and also in and through the words of peace and healing hands of his disciples (see Luke 10.1–9). But the kingdom has yet to come 'with power' (see Chapters 3 and 9).

We may think of the kingdom as finding expression in the Church's life, teaching and fellowship. But this can tempt us into the very big mistake of equating the Church and the kingdom. It is better to think of the kingdom as the Church's goal and meaning, 'what it is moving towards . . . [that] which the Church hopes for, bears witness to, proclaims' (Küng, 1971, p. 96) and for which the Church, we may argue, is 'primarily a foretaste' (Zizioulas, 2008, p. 127). Dorothee Sölle has described the tension this can create along the following lines.

> We can see how both the 'already there' and the 'not yet' belong together if we think of relationships between human beings . . . In them the present 'having' destroys the future being. For example, if I think I know someone completely, if I think that by loving him or her I utterly possess him or her in the present, expect no more of him or her . . . then present security has completely swallowed up future expectation. . . .
>
> When transferred to the church, that amounts to a self-destruction . . . If Christ has become completely the possession of such a community, if there is no longer anything unknown, dark, mysterious, about him, then the Christness is stamped with a false triumphalistic certainty, the boundaries are drawn clearly between within and without, church and world, us and them, and God becomes a household object to make use of. . . . It will no longer expect God. It has become self-sufficient. (Sölle, 1990, pp. 139–40)

The Church must expect more of itself than it already has or does, by thinking more of God. It is not an end in itself but a means, a way. It was created to go beyond itself, as an instrument and servant of God's kingdom.

Further reading

Astley, J., 2010, *SCM Studyguide to Christian Doctrine*, London: SCM Press, Ch. 5.
Barth, K., 1966, *Dogmatics in Outline*, London: SCM Press, Ch. 22.
Dulles, A., 2002, *Models of the Church*, expanded edn, New York: Doubleday.
McGrath, A. E., 2008, *Theology: The Basics*, Oxford: Blackwell, Ch. 7.

Migliore, D. L., 2004, *Faith Seeking Understanding: An Introduction to Christian Theology*, Grand Rapids, MI: Eerdmans, Ch. 11.

Selby, P., 1991, *BeLonging: Challenge to a Tribal Church*, London: SPCK.

Shakespeare, S. and Rayment-Pickard, H., 2006, *The Inclusive God: Reclaiming Theology for an Inclusive Church*, Norwich: Canterbury Press.

3

Forgiveness: Sin, Salvation and Sacraments

One of the criticisms often levelled at the creeds is that they are long on Christian beliefs but short on Christian experience and Christian living, which are precisely the features many would regard as constituting the heart, foundation or source – even the essence – of Christianity.

One valid response to this ticking off might be: 'Well, what do you expect? The clue is in the name. After all, creeds are all about *beliefs*.' On the one hand, however, we might have expected a greater focus on beliefs about Christian experience and the Christian life, including moral and spiritual beliefs. And, on the other hand, a *full* account of the Christian faith certainly must include the Church's teachings about what Christians ought to believe about what to *do* morally (their moral duties and loving behaviour) and religiously (that they should actively trust and hope, and pray and worship, for example). It should also include some reference to what sort of people Christians should *be* in their attitudes, values and dispositions (their spiritual and moral virtues), and in how they should feel (about the world and other people, and about their own hopes and fears and sufferings); and some mention of what experiences of God and God's activity they might expect to have, and should be open to receiving. Without the enrichment of these accompanying 'habitual patterns of behaviour and affective [feeling, emotional] response', Christian belief can seem a very thin affair, made up of mere 'abstract metaphysical claims'[1] remote from the lives, feelings and experiences of most Christians (cf. Cottingham, 2007, p. 35).

All this is undeniable, but I think we can argue that the creeds that have come down to us do not entirely ignore such areas and concerns.

TO DO

Look closely at the Nicene and Apostles' Creeds and try to identify within them any references to Christian life and experience.

Can you think of additional areas of life and experience to which Christians commit themselves? If so, what specific *beliefs* about these things do you think might be included in a Christian creed?

The following phrases from the creeds do at least suggest these wider concerns, some of them quite explicitly:

- (from the Apostles' Creed): 'come to judge', 'the communion of saints', 'the forgiveness of sins', 'life everlasting';
- (from the Nicene Creed): 'for us and for our salvation', 'for our sake', 'he will come again in glory to judge . . . and his kingdom will have no end', 'the Lord, the giver of life, who . . . is worshipped and glorified', 'one baptism for the forgiveness of sins', 'we look for the resurrection . . . and the life of the world to come'. At a further stretch we might include 'in accordance with the Scriptures' and 'who has spoken through the prophets'.

I think that we may identify here some concern about the *Christian experiences* and *feelings* of fellowship with others, forgiveness and salvation (as well as a future judgement), and of hope and longing; and the *Christian behaviours* of worship, praise and sacrament (baptism). The references to new life in God's kingdom, and life itself

---

1 That is, all-embracing philosophical explanations.

as God's gift, also suggest a *Christian spirituality* of acceptance and thankfulness, and a focus not just on experiencing but perhaps also on *living* the kingdom. And those credal references to the Scriptures and to prophecy imply a recognition of the inspiration of both, and of our *experience* or 'reception' of God's revelation through these media.

What is salvation?

Pre-eminent among these elements of Christian experience and life, however, is the key category of salvation. The English words 'save', 'salvation' and 'saviour' are from the Latin words *salvus*, 'safe' and *salvare*, 'to save' (from which we also get the English 'salvage'). The idea of salvation has a secular as well as a theological meaning, with the sense of 'preservation or deliverance from harm, ruin or loss'. In the Bible and Christian theology, salvation has a similar range and is also associated with ideas of 'broadness' and 'wholeness' – being 'made whole'. So the words in the Greek New Testament, *sozo* ('I save') and *soteria* ('salvation'), speak of rescue from danger, and physical or mental healings, as well as spiritual redemption. This broad salvation is what Jesus is all about. His name is itself the Greek form (*Iesous*) of the Hebrew name Joshua, meaning 'Yahweh [usually rendered as The LORD] is salvation'.

The very concept of salvation suggests that there is something amiss in life from which we require to be saved: some disability, inadequacy or restraint from which we need to be released, or some stain, tarnish or contamination from which we need to be cleansed. This is salvation's *starting point*. But all religions also look to a *goal* or aim or destination of this salvation, and some *means* or way by which this goal may be reached and realized (and has been, or will be). These three features constitute the answers to the three-fold question: from what situation are we saved, to and for what end, and by what means? (cf. Clark, 1978, Ch. 4).

In this chapter we shall concentrate mainly on the more concrete, experiential, *human* side of salvation. But although salvation is 'about us', Christian theology regards our role merely as the subjective human appropriation of an objective divine act, in which God takes the initiative in and through Christ to change our situation and our relationship with God. It is God who offers the acceptance and healing to which we must respond with faith. We shall reserve until Chapter 5 our consideration of the major feature of this objective dimension of salvation, the atoning 'work of [God in] Christ', and we shall consider the sanctifying role of the Holy Spirit in Chapter 4. But despite our focus in the present chapter on the human pole of salvation, there are three other aspects of the objective dimension of salvation that we must include here:

- The objective state of alienation from God and bondage to evil *from which* we must be saved.
- The objective processes, such as justification and the offer of acceptance, that are said to result from God's work in Christ to change our situation, and *by which* we may be saved – provided we respond to them subjectively, in faith.
- The objective goal or consummation *to and for which* we are saved, and towards which Christianity directs our hope for salvation.

It is necessary to stress, however, that all of these objective elements are *incomplete* if we do not receive them, respond to them and embrace them. Our subjective response must happen or the circuit will not close and God's power will not flow, and then no one will be healed. 'Salvation is objectively accomplished in Christ; the world has been transformed, . . . and yet these very acts of God in Christ awaken and call forth faith that opens one's life to the new creation that Christ makes possible' (McIntosh, 2008, p. 77).

TO DO

It is likely that you will have been asked at some point in your life, 'Are you saved?' You may also have asked this question of others or of yourself. What do you *now* understand by this question? And how would you respond it?

In particular, and before reading further, see how far you can articulate *your own view* of what it is that Christians are saved from; what they are saved to or for; and how this happens. (I should add that most Christians find this exercise difficult, especially when we try not to use theological or religious jargon that we don't really own for ourselves.)

Salvation from what?

Our creeds talk about the forgiveness of sins, and guilt for sin is the traditional focus of the Christian theology of salvation. The Bible unquestionably identifies sin as a major human problem. According to the dictionaries, sin is a human act. But theologians more often treat it (a) as a *state* of the human heart and will (labelling it 'sinfulness', 'disobedience' or 'rebellion'); but also (b) as a theological 'state of affairs' – the state of being separated from God; and (c) as a label to attach to anything that causes these situations.

'Sin means going astray, failing to find the source of life in our search for life.' Every person's sin is the result of their striving for a fulfilment that merely enriches their own ego 'separated from others and from God' (Pannenberg, 1972, p. 164). Sin's beginnings are described in a number of powerful narratives in chapters 3 to 11 of the book of Genesis. These include the fundamental 'fall' of humankind, together with God's reaction to this primordial sin, both of which are recounted in detail in Genesis 3. Traditionally, this sin of Adam (Hebrew for 'man') came to be thought of as a revolt. It is man's rebellion 'against grace; it is too little for him, he turns away from gratitude', and so 'puts himself . . . behind the back of God's grace' (Barth, 1966, p. 117). This veering away from God 'and toward a finite good', is also frequently interpreted as Adam turning 'in *pride* toward himself. He became . . . incurved back in upon himself, instead of bending toward God' (Inbody, 2005, p. 172). For Augustine (354–430), the source of Adam's sin is this pride, what has been called 'the absolutization of the self'. The result is *guilt*, for which we need forgiveness. But more is required: we also need to respond to the offer of this forgiveness with faith and repentance (that is, through a 'change of mind' and a 'return' to God: cf. Mark 1.15; Acts 2.37–38). For some, however, human guilt is replaced by *shame*. Shame is 'a profound sense of unworthiness' and emptiness, and the denial that God can possibly believe in us, which contrasts markedly with the arrogance of overweening pride (Inbody, 2005, p. 183). In either situation, we really need help.

While we can readily make experiential sense of this analysis, it is a lot more difficult for us than it was for earlier theologians to relate this theology of sin to an original fall that led to God expelling Adam and Eve from the Garden of Eden, and subjecting them to travail and death. This connection had been suggested by the author of Genesis 3, and more explicit links were forged by Paul (see Romans 5.12, 18–19 etc.). Augustine further developed this biblical theme, inflating the fall into an event with even more spectacular effects, including the corruption of the entire human race. As 'we were all in that one man', Augustine claimed that we shared Adam's guilt and therefore also God's just punishment of it, as well as inheriting a corrupt tendency to sin (often but confusingly called 'original sin') and losing our freedom to do anything other than sin. The Reformers Luther and Calvin built on Augustine's view, arguing that the 'image of God' in us (see Genesis 1.26–27), which is perhaps best thought of as our ability to reflect God and form a relationship with God, was either wholly lost or massively deformed by Adam's fall.

Modern accounts of human evolution leave little room for the special creation of a first set of parents for our species, or of an earthly, suffering-free paradise into which they could be born. Although conservative Christians still seek to reclaim the Genesis account as a *historical event* in early human prehistory, more liberal scholars are content to treat it as a grand *mythic story* (see pp. 75, 88) that expresses a theological truth about our present human state, especially our tendency to sin and the chaos and suffering that this inflicts on our species and the whole world. Many theologians are especially uneasy with the claim that we can be guilty of another person's sin, sharing the reservations expressed by Augustine's contemporary Pelagius (who was, however, condemned for his views by the Church). Debate over this moral and theological dilemma may be found even within the Bible: see Exodus 34.6–7; Job 21.17–30; Ezekiel 18.1–4, 19–20.

Biblical accounts that detail the continual sinning of God's people, and God's repeated denunciations, exhortations to repentance and promises of forgiveness, can seem more convincing to many modern ears. We find these topics reflected in (the majority of) the ten commandments, through the words of the prophets and in the teaching of Jesus. In these accounts, unjust and uncaring behaviour *to other human beings* is treated as a sin against God that deserves punishment (see, for example, Exodus 20.12–17; Hosea 4.1–3; 11.1–4, 8–9; Amos 2.6–8; 8.4–6, 9–11; 9.7–8, 13–15; Matthew 25.31–46; Luke 10.25–37; and below pp. 35–6, 65–8).

TO DO

How do *you* understand the idea of 'sin'? What concrete examples of sins and sinners best illustrate such an idea today?

To what extent are people nowadays convinced of their own need to be 'saved from their sins'?

Many argue that sin is not such a potent indictment as it once was. The language of older liturgies such as the Book of Common Prayer, with its insistence on our guilt and unworthiness before God as 'miserable sinners' in whom 'there is no health', may provide an appropriate description of the human condition. But in our own time it simply doesn't capture many people's estimate of themselves, and this is only partly because people are less willing to be made to feel guilty nowadays. Most people *do* believe that there is something wrong with them and about them, and their world. But they don't always express this 'something wrong' in terms of sinfulness. Perhaps sin and its accompanying guilt are not the only things from which we may need to be saved.

When sin becomes the 'one size fits all' metaphor for the human condition, it obscures the rich and important meanings of . . .

other metaphors. According to the Bible, our predicament – what we need deliverance from – is not simply or primarily sin. There are other issues such as bondage, exile, blindness, infirmity, hard-heartedness, and so forth. For these, forgiveness is not the answer. People in bondage need liberation from the Pharaohs who rule their lives, people in exile need to leave Babylon and return home, people who are blind need to see, people who are sick or wounded need healing, people who are outcasts need community. (Borg, 2011, pp. 145–6).

TO DO

So what is wrong with us, in addition to – or even rather than – our sinfulness? Below is a list of things from which we may need salvation. You may want to correct or extend it. Which of the items on the list can you most strongly relate to?

Can you think of biblical texts, or Christian hymns, songs or prayers that address these aspects of our human experience and condition?

- a 'hard, closed heart'
- a lack of meaning and a sense of belonging
- a sense of injustice and unfairness
- a sense of separation, alienation and 'exile'
- a sense of shame
- a sense of worthlessness and being unloved
- being 'lost'
- despair
- disobedience and rebellion
- dying and the fear of death
- excessive pride and self-centred presumption
- mistrust
- overdependence on others

- lack of faith
- selling out to the values of the world, or overconcern with trivial matters
- spiritual 'hunger' and 'thirst'
- spiritual 'illness', 'deadness', 'blindness' or 'deafness'
- spiritual 'bondage' to oppressive powers
- spiritual 'darkness' and ignorance.

(We might widen the last four cases to include real, physical 'hunger', 'bondage' etc. Compare Matthew 5.3–12 with Luke 6.20–23.)

Salvation by what?

In response to the question '*How* are we saved?', Christian theology has taken up the wide range of vivid, metaphors and poetic narratives that it finds in Scripture, and developed them into various 'models' (that is, metaphors that are more systematic and behave more like abstract concepts). It employs these models to describe both the 'objective' effect of God's activity on human beings and the Christian experience of appropriating God's saving activity towards us. They include the following key *models of the process of salvation.*

- *Justification* develops a forensic (legal) image that assumes a trial in a law court, in which a guilty person finds her or himself acquitted and declared innocent or 'righteous' by an act of God's grace, and is thus put 'in the right' before God and restored to her or his relationship over against God (cf. Romans 3).

  Historically, Protestants stressed that this declaration must be received by faith (as trust) alone, and is entirely independent of any 'good works'. Catholics, however, partly because they understood faith more in terms of a mere factual belief about God, were willing to speak of 'faith furnished with love' as what was required from us if we were to appropriate this declaration. They also thought of justification more in terms of a process of regeneration and renewal (that is, actually becoming righteous – see below). The current *Catechism of the Catholic Church* (2000) states that 'with justification, faith, hope and charity are poured into our hearts' as God 'makes us inwardly just by the power of his mercy'; but it adds that 'no one can merit the initial grace of forgiveness and justification' and 'the merits of our good works are gifts of the divine goodness' (§§ 1991–2, 2008–9). One evangelical scholar argues in the following way about the Protestant emphasis on God's declaration of our 'imputed righteousness' (which appeals to yet another metaphor – that of 'reckoning' or entering something into an account – which is derived from the practice of accounting).

> There is indeed a sense in which 'justification' really does make someone 'righteous' – it really does create the 'righteousness', the status-of-being-in-the right, of which it speaks – but 'righteousness' in that lawcourt sense does not mean either 'morally good character' or 'performance of moral good deeds', but 'the status you have when the court has found in your favour'. (Wright, 2009, p. 71)

Justification seems to be down to God's decision to look at us differently, as *through Christ*, and thus our life is 'hidden with Christ in God' (Colossians 3.3). As William Bright's hymn, 'And now, O Father, mindful of the love', develops this theme: 'Look, Father, look on His anointed face, And only look on us as found in Him.'

> God in his mercy has decided to see us in his Son. This is what justification means, that God mercifully sees the sinful life that we have lived and are still living as a thing of the past – dead in Christ's death – and Christ's life as ours. (Cranfield, 2004, p. 46)

In the Christian doctrinal framework, justification is often associated with a special gift of the Holy Spirit that enables a person's regeneration through *sanctification*, literally a 'making holy' (see Chapter 4).

- *Liberation* draws on the metaphor of slavery or imprisonment, and the practice of making an appropriate payment in order to 'redeem' ('buy back') a slave or 'ransom' a prisoner. It carries strong emotional overtones of release and freedom from the chains of sin, and of other powers that spiritually bind us (see pp. 63–5).

- *Healing* is a major part of the Gospel accounts of the ministry of Jesus (and of his disciples too), including exorcisms that drive out the 'evil spirits' that are seen as responsible for physical and mental suffering. Salvation is often presented as a healing deliverance from a fatal illness or long-term disability. The resulting new life is sometimes imaged as an inner peace or even a 'new creation' (Romans 5.1; 2 Corinthians 5.17). It may also be expressed more technically in the language of spiritual 'regeneration' or inner 'transformation', terms that again lead us into the conceptual space occupied by sanctification.

- *Adoption* is another powerful metaphor for receiving, as a gift from outside oneself, a new status, security and relationship of love as members of God's family, and thus 'heirs of God and joint heirs with Christ' (Romans 8.17).

- Where the above models lay their main stress on the objective means that have been provided by God for our salvation, *acceptance* is a spiritual-psychological model that focuses more on our subjective experience and human response. (As such, it can serve as a complement to any of the other models.) By faith we accept that we are accepted, having been forgiven and brought into God's family. Although faith involves both belief and a consequent practical commitment, it is often presented in terms of a simple reaching out in trust to receive God's gift. Both the offer and the acceptance of grace are understood in terms of intensely profound and personal experiences, as Paul Tillich indicates in this famous sermon.

It is as though a voice were saying: 'You are accepted. *You are accepted*, accepted by that which is greater than you, and the name of which you do not know. Do not ask for the name now; perhaps you will find it later. Do not try to do anything now;

perhaps later you will do much. Do not seek for anything; do not perform anything; do not intend anything. *Simply accept the fact that you are accepted!'* If that happens to us, we experience grace. After such an experience we may not be better than before, and we may not believe more than before. But everything is transformed. In that moment, grace conquers sin, and reconciliation bridges the gulf of estrangement. And nothing is demanded of this experience, no religious or moral or intellectual presupposition, nothing but *acceptance.* (Tillich, 1962, pp. 163–4)

TO DO

Which of these models most effectively reflects what matters to you in your Christian experience of salvation? Do any leave you cold, perhaps because you cannot make much sense of the metaphors on which they depend?

To what extent do the following passages illustrate one or other of these dominant images or story-ideas of salvation? Can you find other, or better, examples? Luke 15.11–32; Acts 10.34–35; Romans 3.19–30; 5.12–21; 8.14–23; 1 Corinthians 6.20; Galatians 4.1–9; Ephesians 1.3–14; 2.8–10.

Sacraments

The technical term 'sacrament' appears in the title of this chapter for reasons other than alliteration. Sacraments are ordinary human acts (eating, drinking, washing) and ordinary physical objects (bread, wine, water) that are set apart and recognized as having a special significance. Their role is to symbolize and convey God's grace. According to Augustine, they are 'outward and visible' signs of 'an inward and spiritual grace'. Although they are to be understood as objective acts of God that offer an objective gift of grace, this sacramental grace is said to be something that can only be effectively received and appropriated if the recipient is worthy to do so. This combination of the objective and the subjective ensures that sacramental grace is viewed as a personal act or gift that forms part of a relationship, and not as an impersonal substance that may be conveyed magically or mechanically, or as some divine influence that we are quite unable to resist.

In the Nicene Creed we 'acknowledge one baptism for the forgiveness of sins'. Baptism and the Eucharist are the two 'dominical' sacraments (that is, instituted by Jesus). In the New Testament, baptism is both undergone by Jesus and practised by his followers. It quickly became the rite of initiation into membership of the Church, effecting and symbolizing this change of status theologically and religiously. Theologically, baptism is also associated with the gift of the Holy Spirit, our sharing in the dying and rising of Christ and our spiritual cleansing from sin. The Church eventually affirmed that baptism remitted 'all original and actual guilt' and 'all penalty'.

The sacraments are part (but only part) of the 'by what' of salvation, as human acts that are used by God to change our spiritual status and to convey God's forgiving grace and Spirit (objectively speaking). Subjectively speaking, they change our experience – including how we feel about God and ourselves, including our sins *and* the other factors that tend to alienate us from God. If we were baptized as adults that may well have been our experience then, but it doesn't work like this for infants. In fact all Christians may need to 'revisit' their baptism regularly, continually renewing their vows of commitment in response to God's continuous acceptance.

Salvation to and for what?

For what have we been saved (and are being saved, and will be saved)? What is the aim, goal or 'destination' of Christian salvation?

Put like this, most Christians would answer the question with the single word: 'heaven'. But what is heaven? Many think of it as a place or state beyond this present world, entered into after death and/or after the transformation – or possibly the end – of this whole creation. It may be imagined in terms of a communal relationship with God or an individual participation in God's life, or even an absorption into God's being (see Chapter 9).

But there is also a this-worldly dimension to the 'to what' of salvation. This takes up the Jewish emphasis on peace, well-being, wholeness, healing and welfare that is captured in the Hebrew word *shalom* (which is still used as a salutation). In the New Testament this dimension is expressed in two similar concepts, both of which combine present experience with a future reference.

- The Synoptic Gospels (Matthew, Mark and Luke) mainly look to God's *kingdom*, or rule. As something that is be obeyed and enacted in this world (see pp. 24–5), this kingdom has already dawned through Jesus' ministry, although it is yet to come 'with power' (Mark 1.15; 9.1; Matthew 12.28; Luke 11.20).
- John prefers the concept of 'eternal life', which he presents as the reality of a new depth of life that is experienced now, and will continue past death and God's judgement (John 5.24; 11.25–26).

> In the God who saves we have to do not with mere dreams and hopes, with what might be and one day, we hope, will be; we testify to a gift already received and signs already enacted of that gathering up which is God's will for all things. Already God's realm is inhabited by those who have known God's grace and lived lives empowered by it; already many who were plagued by oppression or sickness of body and mind have experienced release. If it is the case that we are part of a world where pain and alienation still abound and where therefore anything that might reasonably be called salvation is still far off . . . it is nevertheless also and equally true that God's salvation has already drawn near. (Doctrine Commission of the Church of England, 2005, p. 435)

Further reading

Borg, M. J., 2003, *The Heart of Christianity: Rediscovering a Life of Faith*, San Francisco: HarperSanFrancisco, Ch. 9.

Hart, T., 1997, 'Redemption and Fall', in C. Gunton (ed.), *The Cambridge Companion to Christian Doctrine*, Cambridge: Cambridge University Press, Ch. 10.

Inbody, T., 2005, *The Faith of the Christian Church: An Introduction to Theology*, Grand Rapids, MI: Eerdmans, Ch. 7.

McGrath, A. E., 2007, *Christian Theology: An Introduction*, Oxford: Blackwell, Ch. 14.

Stiver, D. R., 2009, *Life Together in the Way of Jesus Christ: An Introduction to Christian Theology*, Waco, TX: Baylor University Press, Ch. 6.

4

Holy Spirit:
Inspiration and Formation

TO DO

Look up 'spirit', 'spiritual', 'spirited' and 'inspiration' in an English dictionary or on the Internet to survey the range of meanings attached to these words.

What connections can you trace between our everyday use of this language and the Bible's references to 'spirit', 'Spirit of God' and 'Holy Spirit', as found in texts like those listed below? How would you characterize the roles taken by God's Spirit in such passages?

Genesis 1.2;* 1 Samuel 16.13; Psalms 33.6; 51.10–12; 104.29–30; Isaiah 42.1–2; 44.1–3; 61.1; Ezekiel 11.19; 37.1–14; Joel 2.28–29; Luke 1.35, 39–42; 2.25–32; 3.15–21; 4.1, 16–21; 24.49; John 3.1–8; 4.24; 14.15–17; 16.7–15; 20.19–23; Acts 2.1–21, 38; Romans 5.3–5; 8.1–17,** 26–27; 1 Corinthians 12—14; Galatians 5.16–25.**

* Here what 'swept over the face of the waters' may be translated as either 'a wind from God' or 'the Spirit of God'.

** Here 'flesh' = human beings in their weakness and selfishness, open to sin.

The English word 'spirit' is used to translate the Hebrew *ruach* in the Old Testament and the Greek *pneuma* in the New Testament. Both these biblical terms also denote the ideas of 'wind' and 'breath', and by extension the (principle of) life. The Spirit of God is associated in the Bible with a very wide range of roles and activities, including:

- artistic skill
- creation and life (and procreation, including the case of Mary)
- empowerment and strength (especially for leadership, healing and proclamation)
- ecstatic states
- forgiveness and holy living
- historical events
- justice
- prophecy
- the sense of God's presence, comfort and conviction
- 'speaking in/with tongues'
- training, inspiring and teaching
- wisdom, understanding and insight.

In the Bible the Spirit is always thought of as God active, giving himself (better, 'Godself') to creation and to the people of God in particular. The Spirit is represented as the living energy of a personal God; it is understood as a more personal manifestation of God's activity rather than as an individual within the Godhead. Yet the Spirit is *divine*, as God is (see Chapter 8). And the Holy Spirit must not be understood 'as a third element, as a thing between God and human beings', for 'Spirit means the personal nearness of God to human beings, as little to be separated from God as the sun's rays are to be separated from the sun itself' (Küng, 1993, p. 125).

In the New Testament, the work of the Spirit is particularly associated with Jesus and the Church. In Luke's Gospel, Jesus' conception and birth, as well as his whole life and ministry, are inspired, empowered and driven by the Spirit. And Luke's second volume, the Acts of the Apostles, has been described as being 'to a considerable extent the story of the operation of the Spirit'. In this book, 'the

Spirit is responsible for appointing missionaries and equipping them for their task'; but its principal gift here is 'prophetic utterance'. Luke regards the apostles' ecstatic speech at Pentecost 'both as some kind of universal vernacular for the proclamation of a worldwide gospel, and also as prophecy' (Evans, 2008, p. 86).

Inspiration

The dictionary defines this word both in a secular way (as 'a sudden brilliant or timely idea') and as a religious term ('the divine influence supposed to have led to the writing of the Bible'). Its etymology can be tracked back to the Latin, *inspirare*, 'to breathe or blow into' (cf. the word 'God-breathed', *theopneustos*, in the late New Testament text 2 Timothy 3.16).

Of authors and texts

Although its central status would have been assumed, the Bible itself is hardly mentioned in the creeds, apart from a passing reference in the Nicene Creed to the fact that Jesus' resurrection was 'in accordance with the [Old Testament] Scriptures' (cf. Hosea 6.2; Luke 24.26–27, 44–47; 1 Corinthians 15.3–4). But the Spirit and the Bible are often closely related in the Christian belief system. This link usually involves acknowledging a supernatural gift or movement of the Spirit in relation to the writing of Scripture, and thus interpreting God as its ultimate author and treating its text – or more usually its supposed source – as inspired (cf. Mark 12.36; Acts 1.16; 4.25; see also 1 Corinthians 12.3). This position is in principle compatible with allowing human frailty in the recipients of this revelation, as they interpret or communicate God's commands, intentions and character. But Christians have adopted a range of positions over this issue.

Sometimes 'errors' in the text could be justified by being tracked back to God; or God's inerrant text was thought to be left open to a wide range of human interpretation at the level of its readers. The

Church father, Origen, in the third century, and the Jewish philos-opher, Philo, in the first century, were among those who assumed a mechanical, dictation model of Scripture. All the same, Origen thought that the Spirit often 'accommodated' the divine message to the author's understanding (a view that the Protestant Reformer, John Calvin, also held later), and that the Scriptures included literal falsehoods implanted by God to make their readers search for a deeper, symbolic sense. And Philo allowed himself great freedom as the interpreter of these dictated Scriptures. Augustine also combined biblical inerrancy with considerable licence in biblical exegesis.

In the late nineteenth and early twentieth centuries a conservative reaction to the growth of critical biblical scholarship and liberal the-ology hardened into the view that God's involvement in revelation must mean that a supernatural bar would have prevented any cor-ruption of its message by its 'hearers' (that is, the prophets, apostles and other 'penultimate authors' of Scripture), and sometimes its later manuscript copiers as well (cf. 2 Peter 1.21). The extreme version of inspiration that is held by *biblical fundamentalists* today involves a mechanical dictation by God to the biblical authors, who as a corol-lary are understood as wholly passive but ultra-accurate secretaries.[1]

The model of *plenary [complete] verbal inspiration* is rather less radical. Many who hold this view claim that the Bible is infallible and its contents inerrant, and therefore incapable of being wrong, neither misleading nor misled and wholly without error – at least in matters of faith and practice. But they may qualify this bold affirma-tion, although the qualifications usually apply only to minor mat-ters or when the Bible pronounces on matters of secular history or science.

The basic criticism of all such views is that God's miraculous oversight potentially undermines human freedom, and that this does not appear to be the way God's relationship with us normally

---

1 A similar interpretation is assumed for the writing of the Qur'an, with the totally illiterate Muhammad receiving this text in a vision from the archangel Gabriel (or 'the Faithful Spirit'), who unforgettably impressed it on his mind. Muhammad then dictated it to his companions. Muhammad is therefore regarded as an involuntary instrument in the process of revelation.

works – and, in the view of many, should work. Some theologians therefore prefer to speak of two complementary activities of authorship – divine and human – that somehow result in the creation of one product. This relationship may be regarded as similar to that between the cooperative, causal influences on 'providential' – or even just 'created' – physical events, which we may treat as being *both* acts of God's *and* scenes of natural causation (see Chapter 7).

More *liberal interpretations* of Scripture tend to retain the concept of inspiration and of the Spirit's role in biblical revelation, but insist that the human minds to which God reveals God's truth and Godself, while 'peculiarly able' to discern the spiritual significance that is being revealed, 'are none the less liable to error and ignorance' (Lampe, 1963, p. 142). Some may even hold that God does no more than 'influence' the biblical authors, who then go on freely to create their 'own work'. Such positions allow the possibility of treating inspiration as a matter of degree, and therefore of locating the prophets, apostles and biblical authors as lying on the same spectrum of inspiration as us – although they are presumably thought of as situated at the opposite end of this spectrum from where most of us would place ourselves.

Of readers

But applying the term inspiration to ourselves is not, perhaps, such an arrogant claim. Historically, Christians have supposed that the work of the Holy Spirit did not only happen in the past, operating back behind the authors of Scripture. God also works within us, as God's Spirit illuminates the spiritual discernment of the reader to understand the message of the Scriptures, even inspiring us to treat these texts *as Scripture*. 'We need the same Spirit to understand the Scripture', Thomas à Kempis wrote in the fifteenth century, 'which enabled the holy men of old to write it.' Calvin agreed, and developed the doctrine of the Spirit's 'illumination' through this interior witness or inner 'testimony' within the readers. He argued that Scripture 'owes the full conviction with which we ought to receive it to the testimony of the Spirit', and this is what enables us to assert that the Bible comes to us 'by the instrumentality of men, from the very mouth of God' (*Institutes of the Christian Religion*, book one, Ch. 7, 5; Ch. 9, 3). He also allowed, however, that the biblical authors might err, if only in details that did not affect doctrine.

Bringing the Spirit's inspiring activity into our own time does not solve all the difficulties, however, because God's action as Spirit has now to be related in some way to the human activities of reaction and interpretation at our end of the proceedings. This is where *our* freedom may operate, with the effect of distorting or even blocking God's intention, unless God decides to control (and therefore remove?) this freedom.

Continuing revelation?

TO DO

What do you make of these different doctrines of the inspiration of Scripture, in respect to both its authors and its readers?

Do you think of God's inspiration as something that continues to influence, or even determine, later theological formulations of the Councils of the Church, or individual theologians or church leaders (e.g. the Pope or the sixteenth-century reformers)?

Do you think of your own thoughts and responses as ever being 'inspired by God' in any sense? If this were to happen, would you regard this as an example of a miraculous intervention by God into your mind?

One of the concerns raised in this exercise is that of balancing the relationship between and contribution to Christian doctrine of (a) Scripture, on the one hand, and of (b) the Church's tradition, on the other. Where Protestants have historically claimed that 'Scripture alone' should be the sole rule and norm of doctrine, Roman Catholic and Eastern Orthodox theology has permitted a greater role to tradition as an additional medium of God's revelation. Yet even on the Protestant view, as we have seen (pp. 5–6), it is difficult to accept the idea that doctrine can simply be 'read off' Scripture. An additional factor is that much biblical material is often framed as hymns, poetry, moral instruction, prophetic declaration, confessions, stories, exhortations, hymns and parables, whose primary purpose is to express or evoke feelings, values and experiences rather than to articulate a theological description. But even where a descriptive account of God's character and activity is directly and wholly explicitly presented in Scripture, it is often couched in figurative or analogical language. Although the creeds retain some of the flavour of their biblical antecedents, on the whole doctrinal thinking much prefers to work in more prosaic, conceptual and reasoned forms of discourse. While the letters of Paul and other writers contain explicit theological assertions and some theological argument, as do other passages (such as John's editorializing comments in his Gospel), these authors were not operating in the same genre or under the same rational constraints as contemporary doctrinal theologians.

Even so, Scripture is always the main source of the raw material for the *content* of the Church's doctrinal reflections; and the authority of doctrine is not solely determined by (purely *formal*) tests of the clarity, plausibility or coherence of its concepts, systems or arguments. Although doctrine may not itself be regarded as inspired, it does build on a biblical foundation that is generally assumed to merit this status. And the doctrine of biblical inspiration remains important in providing Scripture with a 'normative' (standard-setting, rule-making) function in doctrinal debate. Hence sensible appeals to Scripture are entirely proper in discussing doctrine, and the Bible plays an essential and considerable role in any attempt to test doctrinal truth and meaning. However, this is always alongside the criteria of internal logical coherence and consistency with other knowledge, and with the insights of our culture and/or religious experience – and (for some) consistency with the Church's traditions.

Spiritual formation

The indwelling of God's Spirit within the Christian is characteristic of Paul's theology. This 'Spirit-possession' means that 'the believer is already in a measure "spiritual", that is, open to the energy and direction of the Spirit; . . . already in part "spirit", though still living in the "flesh", the natural condition of the present sinful order' (Simpson and Lampe, 1963, p. 393). As indicated in the exercise on p. 42, when Paul refers to human 'flesh' and human 'spirit' he is not reflecting the classical philosophical distinction between two distinct and separable *parts* of a person, with the material body imprisoning our true self, the soul or spirit. For Paul, as for most biblical authors, the human being is an indivisible unity. Paul implies, rather, that there are two aspects of this one indivisible person: in the first case, the person as orientated towards and open to sin; in the second case, as orientated towards and open to God's Spirit. These two aspects conflict, for Christians belong to two different 'worlds' at the same time. 'Whereas the flesh is a source of weakness which lays men and women open to the attacks of sin (Romans 7.5–25), the Spirit is the power of God which supplies the dynamic for the new life' (Caird with Hurst, 1994, p. 206). This 'life-long tension' between flesh and spirit is something that is always present in our lives, and 'it is important to realize that conversion, experience of Spirit, charismatic experience, does not raise the believer above and beyond this conflict – rather the presence and activity of the Spirit sharpens the conflict'. But that is a good thing, for this inner spiritual conflict is 'a sign that the Spirit is having his say in the shaping of character' (Dunn, 1975, pp. 338–9).

> The Spirit dwelling in the believer conforms him to the likeness of Christ (2 Corinthians 3.18; cf. Romans 8.29–30; 12.2) in a progressive process of making him become, or enter into the meaning of, what he has been made by his justification, that is, a son of God. (Simpson and Lampe, 1963, p. 393)

Churches frequently talk these days about the 'formation' of Christians, usually with reference to explicit and recognized educational activities that *form* people's Christian beliefs – together with their Christian dispositions, values and character – into a better shape (it is hoped, a 'more Christian' one). Such distinct and manifest educational processes are important. It is arguable, however, that most Christian formation actually occurs in much more implicit ways, as we learn to be Christlike by receiving from – and contributing to – the Church's worship and fellowship, and the loving behaviour that occurs within and beyond its congregations (see Astley (ed.), 2000, Ch. 2). Some would say that the reason that these implicit processes are so powerful is that when Christians respond in faith to the gospel they open themselves up to God's Spirit, and that it is this Spirit who has the power to mould the Church into the shape of Christ, through and in its acts of praise and love.

> The community and fellowship of Christ which is the church comes about 'in the Holy Spirit'. The Spirit is this fellowship. Faith perceives God in Christ and this perception is itself the power of the Spirit . . . As the church of Christ it is the church of the Holy Spirit. As the fellowship of believers it is creative hope in the world. (Moltmann, 1977, pp. 33–5)

> One definition that Christian theology could offer of 'spirituality' would simply be 'life in the Spirit': life as it is guided by, filled by, impelled by, uplifted by the Spirit; life given over to the Spirit; life exploring the things of the Spirit. Spirituality has to do, a Christian might say, with the Spirit welling up within us, and with all the practices or dispositions that might clear the channel for that upwelling, or stimulate it. To focus on 'spirituality' is, in Christianity, simply to take one way of talking about the whole journey of learning and unlearning by which the Spirit leads people deeper into the life of God. In other words, for Christian theology 'spirituality' is really just another name for Christian life, because Christian life simply *is* life in the Spirit. (Higton, 2008, p. 152)

TO DO

What do you make of these biblical, theological and educational claims about the role of the Holy Spirit in 'Christian formation'? To what extent do they match your experience?

In what ways can the Church best become 'open to the Spirit'? And how is it to judge between God's Spirit and other formative influences (see John 4.1–3)?

Sanctification

To be sanctified is 'to be made holy'. This denotes 'the way upon which [the faithful] are set' (Gunton, 2002, p. 148). For a Christian, sanctification means to become, to be made, more like Christ. The transformative power of this sanctifying formation is traditionally ascribed to the Holy Spirit.

As Chapter 2 implied, holiness is not a characteristic that should be marked by an otherworldly, smug piety. It is a matter of being formed into – 'conformed to' – the character of *Jesus*, which is selfless, self-giving, costly love. This process of deepening our Christian character is sometimes described in terms of growth to maturity in the Christian life. But although this sounds like something that *we* do, drawing on our own resources, theology insists that the initiative, power and direction must always lie with God, and that our spiritual and moral change is in response to – and as we learn from – *God's* activity. For it is God's love that shapes us into Christlikeness, as it also creates and sustains our minds and hearts during their formation. We are, therefore, both made and remade, formed and reformed in God's love by God's love; as on the earthly level we originated and are fashioned in human love by human love.

The effect of sanctification has been characterized as 'created grace'. The process is even viewed in Eastern Christianity as 'divinization'.[2] Unquestionably, sanctification is the closest we can come in this world to the character of Christ, which is the character of God, which is the character of love. The 'fruit of the Spirit' (see 1 Corinthians 13.4–7; Galatians 5.22–23; 2 Peter 1.5–7) is 'a Christ-like character . . . In all of these lists love is pre-eminent, since God is love' (Lane, 2013, p. 149). So there is no end to love.

> The Spirit is at work within us, but He has not yet finished with us. We are not as we once were, but we are not yet what we shall be. . . . The call upon us now is to live, as much as may be, the life of the healed cosmos. We are to live now, as far as we can, the life that will be lived out when all has been made new. . . . We shall frequently be frustrated, for, despite our prayers, healing will often be unforthcoming, and usually be incomplete, and always be temporary, until the healing of all things.
>
> But the Spirit will work within us, to make us the people we were created to be . . . to narrow the gap between what we are and what we are to be. He will beautify us so that more and more, bit by bit, we cede ourselves to sanity, and give our tired world a picture of its coming transfiguration. That is the beauty of holiness, and it is the work of the Holy Spirit. (Lloyd, 2012, pp. 282–3)

Inside out: outside in

As we move through the Bible, from accounts of a general creation of all things to stories of a new creation of inspired and sanctified persons, God's Spirit is portrayed less as an impersonal energy or power and more as God in person, present to and dwelling within the Church. In Christian doctrine too the presence of the Spirit is regarded as essential to every aspect of the Church's work and every dimension of Christian identity, life and character.

---

2 In Eastern Orthodox theology this *theosis* is effected – or initiated – through God the Son's incarnation in Christ (see Chapter 6), as 'the human being is raised to participate in the life of God, and to develop the likeness of God and so become God-like' (Zizioulas, 2008, p. 115).

While there are special gifts (*charismata*, 'grace gifts') of the Spirit, such as 'speaking in tongues' and healing, the New Testament insists that the most fundamental, as well as *the* lasting gift, is the one that is given to all Christians: God's free, forgiving acceptance and empowerment, and especially God's love (1 Corinthians 12—13). This gift is *grace*. 'Grace is not something other than God . . . it is God himself dwelling within people as the Holy Spirit and working in them their identity in Christ' (Norris, 1979, p. 184).

Grace is a gift to Christians as individuals. But it is also – and mainly – given to the whole Church, especially through and in its 'sharing', 'fellowship' or 'community' (Greek, *koinonia*). After his resurrection, this community is created by Jesus returning to his disciples *in the Spirit* (John 14.25–26; 16.5–7; 20.19–23; Luke 24.49; Acts 1.4–5; 2.1–4). And as we have seen, it is this 'Community Spirit' that has the potential to form and transform the Church.

And thereby to transform others? For this gift and this life is not just for the Church. Israel was not 'elected' (called) for its own comfort and privileged status or power but to be a priest-nation to others ('the Gentiles'). Its greater task was to serve the nations and bring them to God (Exodus 19.5–6; Isaiah 49.1–6; 52.13—53.6; Zechariah 8.20–23). The Church has inherited Israel's vocation (1 Peter 2.9). In fact, as William Temple is often quoted as saying, the Church is the only society on earth that exists for those who are *not* its members. So God's Spirit works from the inside out, as we are called to give away God's grace.

Before that, however, we must receive it; and we must do this not only at first hand but also at second hand – from the hands of others. The Bible offers plenty of examples of Gentiles, outsiders and aliens, even pagans, who receive God's Spirit, enlightenment and ministry. Cyrus, king of Persia, is even called God's shepherd (that is, king) and messiah, 'his anointed' (Isaiah 44.28—45.1).

Some theologians argue that 'there is much that the Church can and should learn. And attending to the witness of the Holy Spirit through other faith traditions is an important part of that learning' (Markham, 2008, p. 158). If that is the case, then God's Spirit may be said to come into the Church from a very long way outside: from other faith traditions and perhaps even from those without any religious belief at all. And why not? God creates and keeps in existence many lives that do not recognize or honour him. God is present to us all, even those who are not conscious of that presence. Can the Spirit not also inspire, form and empower others to do the divine will as well, even without their believing in it? Would we then be entitled to say that God works 'through them'?

TO DO

Read the following passages: Numbers 11.26–29; Matthew 7.15–27; 25.31–46; Acts 10.22–28, 44–48.

In what ways are these passages compatible, and in what ways incompatible, with the theology that seems to be implied by John 10.7–10; Acts 4.12; 17.22–31 or Romans 10.8–17?

Some have argued that it is only in terms of the 'fruits' they show in the present world that we may empirically assess any person's religious salvation. For we cannot successfully do so by speculating about transcendent mysteries, such as their future state in which this transformation is expected to be fulfilled, or by inferring the transcendent relationship with God that empowers both this present situation and its future consummation (cf. Okholm and Phillips, 1996, pp. 44, 87).

Further reading

Astley, J., 2010, *SCM Studyguide to Christian Doctrine*, London: SCM Press, pp. 29–36.

Burnaby, J., 1959, *The Belief of Christendom: A Commentary on the Nicene Creed*, London: SPCK, Chs 14 and 15.

Küng, H., 1993, *Credo: The Apostles' Creed Explained for Today*, London: SCM Press, Ch. V.

Lampe, G. W. H., 1977, *God as Spirit*, London: SCM Press.

Markham, I. S., 2008, *Understanding Christian Doctrine*, Oxford: Blackwell, Ch. 9.

Migliore, D. L., 2004, *Faith Seeking Understanding: An Introduction to Christian Theology*, Grand Rapids, MI: Eerdmans, Chs 3 and 10.

Wainwright, G., 1997, 'The Holy Spirit', in C. Gunton (ed.), *The Cambridge Companion to Christian Doctrine*, Cambridge: Cambridge University Press, Ch. 14.

5

Jesus:
Crucified Conqueror?

Where Chapter 3 dealt mainly with the human pole or dimension of God's saving activity, this chapter looks further beyond ourselves and our experience to God's initial objective act, by which we are made whole. In Eastern Christianity, God's saving act is identified primarily with the incarnation (see Chapter 6), and results from the union of our human nature with God and its subsequent transformation. But in Western Christianity, and especially in Protestant theology, the focus of salvation is the death of Christ.

TO DO

Why did you think that Jesus died as he did? Did he have to die?

How significant is the death of Christ within your Christian belief, devotion and living?

The death

Even the enemies of Christianity have mainly agreed with some parts of the Church's creeds: that Jesus was 'crucified', 'died and was buried'. But so were very many others who ran foul of the authorities in the Roman Empire. Crucifixion was a terrible death, but not rare in that place in those days. So no one becomes a Christian simply by believing that Jesus was crucified; you have to believe in something more about the man and about his death. Christians think of Jesus as *Saviour*, and most believe that his death was the key salvific event.

At one level, of course, the event of Jesus' death was as objective as anything could be. The crucifixion could have been videoed, and has been re-enacted many times in plays and films. It has also been represented down through history in paintings, murals and windows, and (in almost every church building) in a symbolic, physical cross or crucifix of wood, metal, stone or brick. But when theologians insist that something happened 'objectively', they intend much more than this. They mean that something happened beyond as well as within this world, beyond yet within and through that tortured, pierced and broken physical body. They mean that there was an 'objective divine act' that involved God, and which changed the relationship between God and human beings – once for all, and for ever.

This is the act, the event, that effects what is called the *atonement* ('at-one-ment'): the making one of two parties in a dispute who are alienated from each other. This is the act that deals with sin, that effects our reconciliation to God and our forgiveness. And it is frequently thought of as helping us overcome the other disabilities and distress that constitute our human lot. This 'something' happened beyond us, outside us, 'in heaven'. But what (if not 'what on earth') could it be, this so-called work of God in Christ? What made that Friday 'Good'?

According to Mark's version of the crucifixion, two other events happened as Jesus 'gave a loud cry and breathed his last'. We must think of the accounts of these additional occurrences as expressing the deeper meaning – the theological interpretation – of Jesus' historical death. They are 'theologically true', 'symbolically true'; that is, they convey a truth that transcends the world and its human history, going beyond it and constituting its spiritual *depth*. First, the curtain of the temple was torn in two; second, the centurion in charge of Jesus' crucifixion exclaimed, 'Truly this man was God's Son' (Mark 15.37–39).

The curtain is what separated the Holy of Holies from the rest of the sanctuary in the Jerusalem temple. Only the high priest could go through it, and then only on the annual Day of Atonement. He did this in order to sprinkle the blood of the sacrificial sin offerings for the priests and the people of Israel over the solid gold 'propitiatory' or 'mercy seat', which rested on top of the 'ark of the covenant'. So the tearing of the curtain reveals that 'the execution of Jesus means that access to the presence of God is now open' (Borg and Crossan, 2008, p. 150) – quite apart from any temple or any Jewish priesthood.

And the centurion's cry means that 'Jesus, executed by the [Roman] empire, is the Son of God. Thus the emperor [who claimed this title for himself] was not.' Jesus was executed as a rebel against Rome, the 'domination system' with which the temple authorities were currently colluding. Jesus suffered and died, then, as 'one who was righteous, condemned by the powers of this world, and who would be vindicated by God'. And, we must keep reiterating, he suffered and died *as he had lived*. His Passion (suffering and death) expressed what lay at the heart of his life, what impassioned him. And that was God, and the kingdom of God – 'God's passion for justice'. It was this passion that 'got him killed . . . *because* of the sin of the world' (Borg and Crossan, 2008, pp. 151, 162).

There are other things that most Christians would want to say about the death of Christ. But few will deny that something like this lies at the foundation of their faith in the cross.

But why did he die? Historians and New Testament scholars respond with a range of historical reasons relating to Jesus' situation. In that context, they say, *anyone* who spoke and acted as Jesus did was asking for trouble, and would likely get it. This is probably also the historical answer to the question, 'Did he have to die?' But to a Christian theologian these question are not – or are not only – historical questions, and they require – or also require – theological answers.

We shall be exploring a range of these answers from the history of doctrine later in this chapter. But we should first look at a few passages from the Gospels.

> **TO DO**
>
> Read the following texts, together with some commentaries on them if possible. What *theological* ideas do they contain that you find helpful and even persuasive in answering the question, 'Why did Jesus (have to) die?'
>
> Matthew 26.47–56; Mark 14.32–42, 60–64; 15.6–15, 26–27, 34; Luke 23.34, 39–43; John 18.33–38; 19.12–16.

The resurrection

The word 'resurrection' appears twice in each of our creeds. The second of these references is to our own future resurrection (see Chapter 9). But the first is to Jesus, who 'on the third day' after his death 'rose again'. Why was that?

> **TO DO**
>
> Why *and how* does the 'Easter message' matter to you? What do you understand by it?

In death on the cross [Jesus] handed over all the meaning of his human life to the Father; this is his prayer. The Father has not accomplished his will through any success of Jesus; Jesus is left with nothing but his love and his obedience, and this is the prayer to the Father to work through his failure.

And, of course, the answer to that prayer is the resurrection. (McCabe, 1987, p. 100)

While Jesus' death on the cross may be the focus of salvation for Christian doctrine, his resurrection is the lens that focuses that cross and the filter that changes its hue. It is the death that is proclaimed as the event in which God acts in Christ, however that is understood. And it is understood in many ways, as we shall see: as a conquest, an example, a ransom or sacrifice, or as some sort of satisfaction or substitution. But it is the resurrection that reveals this disaster as a triumph, this weakness as strength, and this end of life and of all hope as *the* new beginning of both. So whenever the death is preached, the resurrection accompanies it; and alongside the resurrection the death must also be proclaimed.

It is because Jesus lives, and thus because of his resurrection, that 'he is a figure of the present, not simply of the past' (Borg and Crossan, 2008, p. 205). But it is because he died that this resurrection – which is never thought of as the resuscitation of a corpse, but as the gift of a new divine and everlasting form of living – is seen as a new act of God in which God *vindicates* Jesus. In and through this resurrection, then,

> God has said 'yes' to Jesus and 'no' to the powers who executed him. Easter is not about an afterlife or about happy endings. Easter is God's 'yes' to Jesus *against* the powers who killed him. . . . In the words of the earliest and most widespread post-Easter affirmation in the New Testament, *Jesus is Lord*. And if Jesus is Lord, the lords of the world are not. Easter affirms that the domination systems of this world are not of God and that they do not have the final word. (Borg and Crossan, 2008, pp. 205–6)

And the life

Jesus' death and resurrection go together then. But it was not like that for the first disciples. They had to live through their loss and despair, and their own shame and guilt, before everything changed 'on the first day of the week, when the sun had risen' (Mark 16.2). From the perspective of Jesus' *later* followers, however, his death was inevitably seen through and behind his resurrection, and his earthly life through and behind them both.

The resurrection is about *life*, a new life. The risen life of Christ was obviously a different sort of life from what had come before it. This new living was to become the object of prayer and worship, and of confession and proclamation, rather than of historical reminiscence. But it was absolutely essential to Christianity that the risen Christ was thought of as the *same Jesus*, despite these differences. There were already obvious differences during the period of Jesus' resurrection appearances. These included people's difficulties in recognizing him (Luke 24.16; John 20.15), which certainly impacted on their responses and perhaps explains some lingering doubts (Matthew 28.17). But continuity was emphasized by the fact that the risen Christ still bore the marks of his crucifixion (Luke 24.40; John 20.27). Equally significantly, the fact that he is now called 'saviour' expresses continuity with the responses that people made to the 'ministry' (service) of healing, acceptance and forgiveness that Jesus exercised during his earthly life (as in Mark 2.1–17; Luke 19.1–10 and many other passages). There is a continuity, then, of Jesus' salvific power and love. Everything is now new but yet the same. And the post-Easter *experience* of Christian salvation surely includes many elements that would have been familiar to those who were healed and forgiven by Jesus during his earthly ministry.

Unfortunately, in the move away from the New Testament and the creeds and down the centuries of Christian reflection, the salvation Jesus brought to people during his ministry tended to become detached from the salvation he brought by his death – and from his continuing saving role as the risen, ascended, glorified Christ, enthroned at God's hand. It is not that the resurrection overshadowed the death but that the death sometimes overshadowed the life, so that Christian salvation became something more remote from those concrete, deeply felt, life-changing human experiences Jesus had brought to people through the touch of his hands and the power of his words.

Models of atonement

In formulating the 'Christian doctrine of salvation', therefore, the Church to some extent distanced itself from the wide range of accounts of salvation that were available throughout the New Testament, and concentrated on a rather narrower collection of more abstract models and theological explanations.

There was also a tendency for these constructions to take on a life of their own through reflection and argument. Each of the models was developed to provide its own, fuller and more coherent answer to the question that everyone asked about Jesus' death: 'How could it save us?' But in the end, each one produced a restricted answer that could only ever reflect part of the experience, images, narratives and (especially) metaphors of the many-sided reality of Christian salvation, as it was known through the witness of the Bible and by means of Christian worship and spiritual experience. And 'to select a particular metaphor from among those available . . . and to develop it in isolation from and at the expense of others, is to risk a partial and inadequate grasp on the reality of redemption' (Hart, 1997, p. 190).

Perhaps this is why no one model or theory of the atonement has ever been declared a dogma; that is, a doctrine regarded as divinely revealed and therefore binding on the whole Church. So we might do well to stick with the variety ourselves. We should try to give each model its due, as far as we can, while expecting that each will have its own weaknesses. We should also recognize that the differences across this range of models may appeal to different people's different experiences of God's salvation and their perceptions of Christ's role within it.

TO DO

Reflect on the words of your favourite hymns and songs for Passiontide and Easter. And explore something of the range of visual images of Jesus' death and resurrection in local churches, in art galleries or on the Internet.

Which of these images, metaphors and themes do you find most powerful and compelling, and why?

Victory

The Lutheran theologian Gustav Aulén described this model as the 'classic' or 'dramatic' view.

> Its central theme is the idea of the Atonement as a Divine conflict and victory; Christ – Christus Victor – fights against and triumphs over the evil powers of the world, the 'tyrants' under which mankind is in bondage and suffering, and in Him God reconciles the world to Himself. . . .
>
> The work of Atonement is accomplished by God Himself in Christ . . . There is no satisfaction of God's justice, for the relation of man to God is viewed in the light, not of merit and justice, but of grace. (Aulén, 1970, pp. 4, 145–6)

Christians enter into Christ's victory by putting themselves under their conquering Lord's protection.

This view developed out of the victory motif associated with Christ's death in the New Testament (cf. Colossians 2.15; Hebrews 2.14–15), and from the more general idea of a cosmic battle that was being waged throughout Jesus' ministry with the powers of evil, which often involved exorcisms and is especially vividly detailed in Mark's Gospel (e.g. Mark 1.23–27; 9.20–29; cf. John 16.33). While the classic view treats sin 'as an objective power . . . and the Atonement as the triumph of God over sin, death, and the devil' (Aulén, 1970, p. 147), modern theology has 'demythologized' this model by reinterpreting it so that it can better speak to us today. So contemporary theologies of liberation might interpret the evil spiritual powers as the selfish and perverted spirituality 'at the core of . . . institutions and structures' that dominate our society (Wink, 1998, p. 4, cf. p. 24). Walter Wink argues, however, that:

> One does not become free from the Powers by defeating them in a frontal attack. Rather, one dies to their control . . . (Luke 17.33). Here also the cross is the model: we are liberated, not by striking back at what enslaves us – for even striking back reveals that we are still controlled by violence – but by a willingness to die rather than submit to its command. (p. 93)

Sacrifice and scapegoat

Sacrifice is another strong New Testament theme associated with the death of Christ (cf. Romans 3.25; Ephesians 5.2; Hebrews 9.11–28; 10.11–23; 1 John 4.10; see also Mark 14.22–25). The recurrent sacrifices of animals in the Jerusalem temple, and especially the sin and guilt offerings, were seen essentially as gifts, returning the animal's life to God and thereby providing a means for restoring the people's relationship with God. The death of Christ, the 'lamb of God' (John 1.29; 1 Corinthians 5.7; Revelation 5.11–14), was soon seen as a superior sacrifice, which had been offered – and only needed to be offered – once but has permanently transformed our relationship with God. This sacrifice was thought of as taking away the sins *of the world*. It was offered on our behalf, to purge our guilt, by a Christ who came to be thought of both as victim and as the one who sacrifices the victim, offering himself (in union with us) to himself (in union with God). 'Thus he is both the priest, himself making the offering, and the oblation . . . This was the supreme sacrifice, and the true sacrifice' (Augustine, *City of God*, Book 10, Ch. 20, p. 401).

Another of the key sacrifices in Hebrew religion was associated with the 'scapegoat', which was sent into the desert carrying all the sins of Israel (Leviticus 16.21–22; cf. 2 Corinthians 5.21). The French scholar René Girard argues that scapegoating was a universal phenomenon in ancient cultures, but that its rationale was undermined by the account of an innocent Jesus, who dies as a scapegoat but is resurrected by God and returns to forgive. His non-violence breaks the cycle of violence and brings peace.

Ransom

This New Testament metaphor (cf. Mark 10.45; 1 Timothy 2.6) is related to metaphors of redeeming or buying back slaves (cf. 1 Corinthians 6.20; 7.23; Hebrews 2.14–15). It was developed in the second century and later, in terms of a payment to the devil or even as a deception of the devil – who is persuaded to give up his power over us (e.g. Origen) or is fooled into losing it (e.g. the sixth-century Gregory of Nyssa, who thought of the devil as behaving like a sea-monster that killed itself by attacking the hook of Christ's sinless humanity).

Example

The previous models are highly objective, postulating a cosmic mythological event 'in heaven' that occurs as the transcendent accompaniment to Jesus' death on earth. But some theologians have laid more stress on our response, principally our response to the exhibition in Christ's crucifixion of the supreme example of God's love (cf. John 15.13; Romans 5.6–8). The 'atoning sacrifice' of Christ is here envisioned as God's act of supreme love (1 John 4.9–11). Like the centurion at the foot of the cross, we are converted when we see how he dies. As Isaac Watts' well-known hymn puts it, it is when I 'survey the wondrous cross on which the Prince of Glory died' that I 'pour contempt on all my pride'.

On the cross, which is 'the ultimate sign of man's hatred', the love of God accepts humankind in its 'most extreme sinfulness and bitter enmity' (Lampe, 1966, p. 190). God's ideal love both motivates us and empowers us to emulate this love. Peter Abelard (1074–1142) stressed this 'exemplary' aspect of the atonement, and later theologians took it further. The model has the advantage of treating Christ's death in continuity with his life, which is explicitly seen as an example to follow in John 13.14–15; 2 Corinthians 8.9; Ephesians 5.1–2 and Philippians 2.5–8. Reconciliation comes as a result of our effort to follow Jesus' example. Modern interpretations of Jesus as being primarily a teacher of true knowledge about ourselves (which is seen as a form of salvation), and the cross as symbolizing our death to ignorance, would also come under this model.

The disadvantages of this model, in the eyes of many theologians, is that such a subjective view does not deal (objectively) with the (objective) negative consequences of our sin, bondage or rebellion. Forgiveness is not enough, they say, without some reparation (which means to 'restore' or 'set right', from the verb, 'to repair') – especially some making amends for wrongs committed, some healings of wounds or restoring of losses. 'To say that God could simply forgive . . . may be true abstractly, but it would trivialize that which causes the problem in the first place . . . the conditions that created the offence' (Gunton, 2002, p. 76). This subjective model also finds it hard to hold on to claims about the unique status of Christ's death.

> It tends to see Christ as an example to emulate but not [as] making a unique sacrifice for humankind. In the New Testament, it seems more evident that the latter is the basis for the former, rather than being optional. (Stiver, 2009, p. 323)

The question that such criticisms must face, however, is whether the other atonement models can offer a *religiously* plausible account of how this sacrifice, or any other objective act of God, effects reconciliation and deals with sin. We should reflect on this as we review two other options. (For some further reflections, see Astley, 2010, pp. 129–33.)

Satisfaction

From its formulation in 1098, Anselm of Canterbury's atonement theory came to dominate Western Christianity. It provided another highly objective model, this time stressing the outrage and offence that had been caused to God's majesty by human sin. Anselm argued that this was so great that it could only be 'satisfied' by a God-Man, for 'only God could pay for such a crime, but only an innocent human could offer it' (Stiver, 2009, p. 319) – in Anselm's own words, this is a satisfaction that 'none but God can make' yet 'none but man ought to do' (*Cur Deus Homo?*, book two, 6). So Christ suffers the punishment for our sin *vicariously*; that is, as something 'done for another'.

Although Anselm understood God's act in sending his Son (as an offering for us) as an act of love, the model is often criticized as presenting atonement as an impersonal, abstract legal transaction by which even God is bound.

Substitution

In the hands of John Calvin, Anselm's 'legal' or 'judicial' model was developed in terms of the idea of objective justice that pertained in the sixteenth century. In the divine law court a price must be paid before God can forgive the sin of the world; but that price is so great that God himself must pay the price by providing the substitute, through an act of *penal substitution*, to bear both the sin and the punishment. Christ, therefore, 'took the punishment upon himself, and bore what by the just judgement of God was impending over sinners; with his own blood expiated the sins which rendered them hateful to God, by this expiation satisfied and duly propitiated God the Father' (*Institutes of the Christian Religion*, book two, Ch. 16, 2).

> Whereas the restoration of order is central for Anselm, Calvin is more concerned with the vindication of the law . . . Anselm's Christ pays our debts, Calvin's Christ bears our punishment. Instead of compensation for personal injury (Anselm), the cross is punishment for violation of the law (Calvin). (Inbody, 2005, p. 222)

For many this became *the* way of understanding Paul's words in 2 Corinthians 5.21: 'For our sake he made him to be sin who knew no sin, so that in him we might become the righteousness of God' (cf. also 1 Peter 2.24; 3.18). The model also picks up the Old Testament theme of Israel as God's suffering servant (see, for example, Isaiah 53.5–6).

Substitution is still the dominant model in conservative Protestant circles. Unfortunately it also can give the impression that it depends on an abstract principle that requires to be honoured, limiting God's freedom of action. Although both of these legal models may satisfy the demand for objectivity – that 'something is objectively done' to make God and humanity one – they both remain strangely abstract and formal accounts. They also focus almost entirely on the death of Christ, sometimes with little reference to either his earthly ministry or his resurrection, whereas some of the other models are flexible enough fully to incorporate these elements. The substitution model also concentrates on punishment, which is here treated as retributive (rather than restorative or reformatory, which many today would consider to be the only acceptable justifications for any punishment).

TO DO

Look back at your responses to the first exercise in this chapter. Has this survey of atonement models changed how you would now respond to any of those questions?

Which of the atonement models do you find helpful in understanding the effects of Christ's death and which do you find unhelpful – and why?

Thinking through the atonement

While each of these models offers some insight, all have shortcomings.

A recurrent problem seems to be the danger of interpreting the cross as part of some cosmic, mysterious *transaction* that is being played out in another, transcendent realm between God and Christ (Father and Son), and which includes sin, humanity in general and possibly the devil. Focusing on the physical, real crucifixion can bring us back down to earth. This concrete event was the location of Jesus' real suffering and death. And if the incarnation means anything, it means that this was also the place of *God's* suffering. In Martin Luther's phrase, the crucified Jesus was also 'the crucified God'. The love of Christ, which is the love of God, was and is *costly*. But it was and is a costly sacrifice that broke and breaks the vicious circle of violence – and of punishment for sin? – by somehow absorbing human evil, even unto death. So Christ 'reigns from the tree', and death and human sin can no longer have dominion over us. And that changes everything.

TO DO

What sense, if any, can you make of these metaphors of 'absorbing evil', and of its no longer 'having dominion' over us? How can the *death* of Christ effect these things?

'The cross and resurrection of Jesus Christ inscribes deeply into human history the truth that God's compassion is greater than the murderous passions of our world, . . . that God's way of life is greater than our way of death' (Migliore, 2004, p. 191). As we have seen, the theme of the power of *non-violence* has been picked up within various models of the atonement. In this scenario, 'God effectively overcomes the enemy by refusing to use its weapons' (Gunton, 2002, p. 74). These claims seem to point to moral and spiritual truths, and to their effects on humans, their effects on us. Is this how we (humans) really think (about power and greatness), and is this how we really respond to the Jesus who allows himself to be killed?

'If God is for us, who is against us?' (Romans 8.31). *That* is surely the heart of the gospel of the cross; and it can bring salvation if we find ourselves, in our own turn, 'for' this God. Maybe the cross can change not only our relationship with God but also our relationship with the 'false gods' of violence, merit, status, suffering and death – powerful realities within our world that often hold us in their power, psychologically and spiritually. It is a moot point whether we should consider this second change of relationship as 'objective' or 'merely subjective'. As counsellors know, how we feel about another or a relationship can trump any analysis of 'what is really true' about them. Is it the same in our relationship with God?

Yet there must always be a concern for 'how things really are' and whether our hopes and feelings can be judged to be 'realistic' in the light of this. And the objective claim we must never give up is that God is for us. This is what matters (= is important) 'objectively', as a fact; but it only matters (= concerns us; is significant for us) 'subjectively' when we come to believe it.

Further reading

Lloyd, M., 2012, *Café Theology: Exploring Love, the Universe and Everything*, London: St Paul's Theological Centre, Chs 5 and 6.

Markham, I. S., 2008, *Understanding Christian Doctrine*, Oxford: Blackwell, Ch. 8.

McGrath, A. E., 2007, *Christian Theology: An Introduction*, Oxford: Blackwell, Ch. 13.

McGrath, A. E., 2008, *Theology: The Basics*, Oxford: Blackwell, Ch. 5.

Stiver, D. R., 2009, *Life Together in the Way of Jesus Christ: An Introduction to Christian Theology*, Waco, TX: Baylor University Press, pp. 307–25.

6

Jesus:
Man for Us, God for Us?

Church pulpits may still occasionally be found with an engraved message strategically placed to catch the preacher's attention. It is often the text of John 12.21 – the request of 'some Greeks' to the Apostle Philip, rendered in the Authorized Version as 'We would see Jesus'. Perhaps these words have stopped one or two of the more sensitive preachers in their tracks.

Whatever else Christianity is about, it is about Jesus. 'It is not possible to define an essence of Christianity beyond saying that the faith relates to Christ, either in historical continuity or through religious experience or both' (Smart, 1979, p. 128). 'Everything can be called Christian which in theory and practice has an explicit positive reference to Jesus Christ' (Küng, 1977, p. 125). These criteria cover a very wide field, of course; and both Christian doctrine and Christian piety agree that it matters *how* we see Jesus.

An incident in Mark's Gospel that is said to have occurred around Caesarea Philippi marked a pivotal moment in Jesus' teaching and ministry. It was provoked by Jesus' question to his disciples, 'Who do you say that I am?' (Mark 8.29).

TO DO

How would you answer this question, in your own time and place?

Select (a) one passage of Scripture and (b) one hymn or song that best sum up how you see Jesus. Attempt to do the same for (c) images or depictions (paintings, sculptures, stained-glass windows etc.). (You might try searching the Internet to widen the possibilities, for example by looking at https://en.wikipedia.org/wiki/Depiction_of_Jesus.) What is it in these words and pictures that *particularly* expresses your view of Christ?

Jesus or Christ?

Does it matter that we often use the two words 'Jesus' and 'Christ' without discriminating between them? Scholars have distinguished between the 'Jesus of history' and 'the Christ of faith'; that is, between the 'critical study of the story of Jesus of Nazareth' and 'the development of Christian doctrine' about him. But to treat these two categories as separate and opposing perspectives 'is likely to distort', for:

> we know Jesus of Nazareth only through the tradition of the church with its varied theological colouring . . . some elements in which may be more close to the person who gave rise to Christianity than others, [and] it is now impossible to go back in any substantial detail to an original historical figure and recreate the story all over again in a different way. (Bowden, 1983, p. 306)

Despite recent opinion polls showing that 40 per cent of the population in England don't think that Jesus is a real person, most scholars agree that he *was* a historical figure. However, we mainly know about him through New Testament documents that were written by those who had already responded to him as the Christ of their faith and the resurrected Lord of their worship and longing. And if Jesus is going to be important to us, *religiously and theologically*, then a mere 'historical' reconstruction that strips away anything religious or theological in our view of him will not meet our (religious and theological) needs (see Johnson, 2010, pp. 553–6).

This sort of interpretation goes all the way down. It takes us past the written accounts in the Gospels, the preaching of the apostles in Acts, and the earliest confessions of faith, prayers and other relevant material in the epistles: right back down to the interpretations and responses of Jesus' first disciples – and of others too (see Mark 8.27–28). Although there are many common features to these interpretations, there are also some major differences of perspective and understanding, even though they all confess Jesus as their Lord.

But 'Christology' (the doctrine of the person of Christ) is not just a second-hand term denoting other people's views of Jesus Christ. We need a Christology of our own that represents our reflections on the meaning of Jesus – his significance for *our* faith. In developing our own views we shall inevitably be rather selective in our own thinking about Christ and in our use of the biblical material – just like all the theologians and all the Christians who went before us.

TO DO

Read *all* the following texts. Then select just *four* that you find most illuminating and try to summarize the 'picture of Jesus' or 'faith in Jesus Christ' that each of those four texts express.

Matthew 12.15–21; 28.16–20; Mark 1.9–11; 2.1–12; 9.2–13; 13.32; 14.61–64; 15.26–32; Luke 2.10–11; 4.16–25; 24.25–27; John 1.1–18; 10.31–39; 13.8–13; Acts 2.22–36; 3.13–15; 10.34–43; Romans 1.1–6; 1 Corinthians 1.22–24; Philippians 2.5–11; Hebrews 1.1–4; 2.9; 4.14–16; Revelation 1.12–18; 22.12, 16.

You will have noticed the many different titles that are applied to Jesus and how Jesus refers to himself. New Testament titles for Jesus include Prophet, Messiah,[1] Son of David, Son of Man,[2] Son of God (or just Son). There is also some variety in the way these titles are applied and in their apparent meaning, as well as in the other claims that are made both of and by Jesus. One New Testament scholar writes positively about this variety, arguing that 'from the first the significance of Christ could only be apprehended by a diversity of formulations which though not always strictly compatible with each other were not regarded as rendering each other invalid' (Dunn, 1989, p. 267). Yet despite the diversity, most would agree with another scholar that at the heart of New Testament Christology lies 'the claim that Jesus is the definitive manifestation of God to humanity' – while allowing that individual authors have different ways of expressing this, emphasizing 'different aspects', and that 'not all of these conceptions were maintained' in the later reflections of the Church (Watson, 2010, p. 114).

TO DO

A first-century Christian text suggested to its readers that 'we ought to so think of Jesus Christ as of God' (*2 Clement* 1.1). How do you react to this?

Review the sections of the creeds that refer to Jesus Christ. How do the Apostles' and Nicene Creeds respond to the question, 'Who do you say that I am?'? Which of the words or phrases in these credal affirmations are likely to raise difficulties for Christians today?

Clearly the Nicene Creed gives a much fuller exposition of orthodox Christology, at least in respect to who Jesus is (Jesus' 'nature'). The two

---

1 'The anointed one'. This is *Christos* in Greek, which gives us the English word 'Christ'. Although originally a title, it very soon morphed into what almost amounted to Jesus' surname, as 'Jesus, the Christ' became 'Jesus Christ'. Something is usually lost when a title becomes a name.

2 This is Jesus' main self-characterization. Its meaning on his own lips remains disputed among scholars.

creeds more or less agree, however, about the 'story of Jesus' – what happens to him and what he will eventually do. So let us look first at this Christological *story*.

Story-Christology

I should say at the outset that I am not using the word 'story' here in the sense of an intended fiction or imaginary tale but to refer to a *narrative* (an account of a sequence of connected events) that is normally presented as true. The material about Jesus in the Bible is mainly couched in dynamic, story form. Most of these stories, of course, are this-worldly, historical narratives – as Jesus was a this-worldly, human figure. So we have stories about his birth and ministry and very extensive accounts of his death.

But the Bible also contains less earthly narratives of events that are, at least partly, played out in another, heavenly dimension. These 'acts of God' represent the meaning behind the this-worldly events and reveal how God is engaged with and in them. (Scholars refer to such narratives as *myths*, which does not imply that they are untruths but simply categorizes them as powerful stories about God or the gods interacting with our world.)

It is often said that these cosmic biblical stories form the basis of the Church's doctrines. We might argue that doctrine appears to be better suited to painting conceptual 'portraits', offering static portrayals of God's character or nature, but that it is not always very successful at rendering conceptual narratives or 'doctrinal movies' of God's activity. Perhaps this is because stories are less easily transposed into the abstract mode of theological ideas, as their dramatic meaning is so closely wedded to the concrete and the literal. We might take art as an analogy. Sometimes abstract art doesn't look much like – or even anything like – the 'subject' the artist contends it is about or we think it is about. But mostly we can see some connection, and then (perhaps) it 'works' for us; that is, it expresses something, sometimes very powerfully. But in order for *films* to express abstract ideas, such as moral values or ideals, they must remain fairly concrete and human – or we shall miss the point of them altogether. So there aren't many 'abstract movies' around, while there are plenty of abstract paintings and sculptures. Stories are somehow always 'set in concrete', we might say (but perhaps we'd better not . . .).

Anyway, our creeds are chock-full of narratives about Jesus. He is conceived, born, suffered, died, buried – all on our this-worldly plane. You could make a movie of this earthly (hi)story, and there are plenty to choose from of course. But the cosmic, divine action-story is present in the creeds too:

- '[conceived] by the Holy Spirit, [born] of the Virgin Mary';
- 'begotten, not made';[3]
- 'came down from heaven'; 'was incarnate', 'was made man';
- 'descended to the dead', 'rose again', 'ascended into heaven';
- 'will come [again in glory] to judge' all humankind.

It is possible to construct some sort of 'flow chart' from many of these narrative elements, showing a movement from God to humanity and from heaven to earth and back again to heaven and God. As is often the case with theological language, however, it is important not to take these 'descents' and 'ascents' literally, as if they were movements in our physical space; for they express metaphorically the interactions between worldly and Godly realities. Nonetheless these stories speak powerfully of a sequence – a moving picture – rather than a snapshot. They also present us with a changing Christ rather than an unchanging one.

Some of the earliest Christological stories were never developed further into orthodox Christian doctrines. This was the case with *adoptionism*, in which the man Jesus was thought of as exalted to divine status at his baptism or resurrection (cf. Mark 1.11; Acts 2.36; 3.13–15). And it is also largely the case with the idea of the *kenoticism* ('self-emptying') of a pre-existent, heavenly Christ

---

3 'Begotten' means procreated or generated. Parents 'beget' a child of the same kind as themselves, whereas anything that is 'made' has a being that is different from its maker.

who gives up his divine status for earthly humiliation and service, before it is later restored by God (cf. Philippians 2.5–11). The Christological narrative that was developed most fully had been hinted at by Paul and expounded much more explicitly in John's Gospel (John 1.1–18; 16.28; 17.5). Here the divine Son or Logos ('Word', God's self-expression) leaves heaven and becomes fully *incarnated* (enfleshed, embodied) in the real human life of Jesus, while remaining in the same relationship with his Father. Of our two creeds, only the Nicene uses this I-word: affirming that the Lord Jesus Christ 'was incarnate from the Holy Spirit and the Virgin Mary', and 'was made man'.

Nature-Christology

It is tempting to call this section 'Stuff-Christology', although that doesn't sound quite grand enough. 'Substance-Christology' would be an alternative heading. Where the first type of Christology (story-Christology) focuses on verbs, nature-Christology prefers nouns. Only our Nicene Creed expresses the person of Christ in this way – but it does it in spades. Here Jesus Christ is:

- 'the only Son of God, eternally begotten';
- 'God from God, Light from Light, true God from true God';
- 'of one Being with the Father'.

Much of this language was first hammered out at the Council of Nicaea in 325 and later enshrined in the creed at the Council of Constantinople (381). (These were the first two 'ecumenical councils' of the Christian Church.) It embodies the key Greek term *homoousios*, which means that Christ was 'of the same substance' as – translated in our own version as 'of one Being with' – God the Father. This word can be found nowhere in Scripture but was proposed, originally by the Emperor Constantine in fact but championed by the great Athanasius (*c.* 296–377), to help combat the view taught by the heretical Arius (250–336). Arius had argued that Christ was subordinate to God, a sort of demi-god or supreme creature who was only *like* God ('of like substance') – in other words, that Christ was not fully divine.

TO DO

Why did, and does, this matter? Does it matter to *you* – and if so, why?

How would you attempt to explain how *the man* Jesus can be 'fully divine'?

Our Nicene Creed did not bring an end to discussion over the person of Christ, not by a long way. Claiming *full divinity* for Christ could only be half of the task of Christology, as on its own it could lead to a qualification or disparagement of his humanity. Whatever we think of the convoluted arguments and disagreements in the history of Christology, we must keep in mind that debates over such issues mattered to people. Historically, they mattered because of the two principles at stake over the significance of Jesus.

> The first was that because only God can save, Jesus' reality as God in action must in some way be preserved . . . The second . . . that unless Jesus is fully human salvation is again not guaranteed . . . that if human being is to be restored to its right condition, the change must happen from within, taking account of human freedom rather than forcing people into an alien pattern. (Gunton, 2002, pp. 86–7)

To put it differently: to guarantee that Christ was really the saviour of the human race, he had to be fully human *and* fully divine. For yes, of course, only God can save; yet God can only truly come to us to do so if he becomes completely one with us, one *of* us.

The risk of emphasizing the importance of one of the component natures of Jesus Christ at the expense of the other bulks very large in the doctrine of the person of Christ. This is especially the case once we have moved away from the stories and begun to explain Jesus in terms of stuff (that is, natures). Even when two stories about the same person appear to conflict they can often still both be told, though perhaps with reference to different contexts or from different perspectives (as with the 'complementarity' of understanding electrons – or their behaviour – as akin to both 'particles' and 'waves'). But the imagery of stuff leads to thoughts of weight, and under the influence of this image we tend to think of the two parts of Christ 'getting out of equilibrium', as one is given more 'weight' than the other. Then the 'balance' tips one way, so that Christ's divinity gets emphasized at the expense of his humanity, or vice versa if it tilts the other way. Nature-Christology also raises the difficulty of envisioning 'two layers of being that have to be joined together' – that is, two 'storeys'; and this has led some theologians to revert to 'two stories' of man-language and God-language (Robinson, 1973, pp. 116–17).

However Christology is expressed, overemphasizing Christ's divinity can make the incarnation appear a fraud, leading to the objection: 'So he isn't really human at all!' Whereas shifting the emphasis in the opposite direction seems to make the opposite mistake of denying that Jesus' life and work is fully 'of God' – in which case, whatever we find in Christ, it is not truly *God's* love, forgiveness, presence and power.

So over the next few centuries the *full humanity* of Christ had to be affirmed as well, to 'restore the balance', because unbalance leads to heresy. And finally a *true unity* of Christ's two natures had to be defined, in case the two portions 'fell apart' and the one person of Christ ceased to be one person at all. Those who prefer more mobile metaphors might say that this enabled the Church to keep its Christological vehicle on the road, steering a steady middle-of-the-road course between two extremes – the two road verges that mark the road's boundaries, beyond which lies the wild country of heresy.

For these reasons, then, Christ became interpreted as 'one person in two natures', in Pope Leo's phrase. In 451 the Council of Chalcedon produced 'a definition' (not a creed) that has ever since defined the orthodox doctrine of the person of Christ in the following terms:

- of one substance with the Father (in his Godhead), and therefore truly God, *but also*
- of one substance with us (in his humanity), and therefore truly human,
- with both natures (substances) retaining their different qualities 'without confusion, without change, without division, without separation'.

Yet this does *not* mean that we have two persons, for there is only 'one subject, one agent or actor, one person' of Jesus Christ. And he is, without any separation or division, both 'the eternal Son of God and the man of Nazareth' (Burnaby, 1959, p. 79).

> The unique and altogether singular event of the Incarnation of the Son of God does not mean that Jesus Christ is part God and part man, nor does it imply that he is the result of a confused mixture of the divine and the human. He became truly man while remaining truly God. (*Catechism of the Catholic Church*, 2000, § 464)

'Well, how does that work then?', we may ask; but Chalcedon won't give us an answer. For the Chalcedonian Definition doesn't *explain* how it works. It doesn't explain Christ – it only *defines* him, as two natures in one person. (And if Chalcedon's more detailed account doesn't explain or resolve this paradox – this apparent contradiction – of the 'God-Man', then the Nicene Creed offers even less of an explanation.) 'Chalcedon sought only to safeguard the apostolic faith: the conviction that Jesus of Nazareth, in his life and death, was and is "God with us"' (Loughlin, 1991, p. 189). Indeed, this theologian prefers to treat the Definition as 'a *grammatical rule* for how one should and should not speak of Jesus and God together and apart' (p. 188). It tells us how to talk of Christ: that we must speak of him as God *and* speak of him as a man. It does not tell us *how* this is so. (Which looks as though we are being asked to go back to the 'two stories' . . .)

There have been other ways, however, of resolving the paradox of claiming that Jesus Christ is both human and divine, including options that, while appealing strongly to some theologians, have been vigorously condemned by others.

Functional Christologies

To focus on Jesus' nature(s) is to focus on his being, substance or essence – in a technical term, it is to stress his 'ontology'. Some have preferred to return to a more dynamic way of thinking about Jesus, but instead of reclaiming a narrative approach – particularly if it involves narratives about where Jesus 'came from' and has 'moved to' – they have concentrated on what Jesus did and does; that is, his activity or 'function'. This may be thought of as being more biblical, if the question 'Who is Christ?' meant 'first of all, "What is his function?"' (Cullmann, 1963, p. 4). In any case, we have moved back once more to verbs.

So our question now becomes: 'What matters to us about what Jesus *does*?' Clearly, Jesus forgives and saves/heals (in the different ways outlined in Chapters 3 and 5). He also reveals God (especially God's character) to us, and he loves his life out for us.

> If categories of person and relationship replace categories of substance, the incarnation can be described in language closer to the Gospel story. Unlike classical metaphysics, a thing can be known by what it *does* instead of what it *is*. This is especially true of persons, both divine and human, whose 'natures' are their relationships and acts, not their fixed substances. (Inbody, 2005, p. 209)

Might we say, then, that Jesus' forgiving, loving, healing and revealing are continuous with, or one-and-the-same as, the forgiving, loving, healing and revealing of God? And if so, can we add that Jesus' acts are *wholly* (in the sense of truly, authentically) God's acts, although they do not exhaust *the whole of* God's activity? 'Wholly God' but not the 'whole of God'? As Inbody continues, 'Jesus' activity, power, and purpose were his own and God's, even though this was not the whole of the divine activity in the creation.' Once more – and not for the last time in this book – we are confronted by issues of identity and continuity.

To appeal to another metaphor (cf. pp. 16–17, 35, 62, 104–6), the light emitted from the sun is one and the same light as that which arrives to illuminate the earth, in that there is a causal continuity between the two and both are of the same quality – at least in terms of their spectra of wavelengths (before our atmosphere intervenes, anyway). But we would not survive long if all the electromagnetic radiation that fell on the earth possessed the same energy it had when it was emitted from the surface of the sun. This model also suggests that God's light may be sent out in other directions, through 'other channels', illuminating other planets as well.

TO DO

What are the (a) strengths and (b) weaknesses of a functional Christology?

Two criticisms of such views might occur to you. First of all, one would have to admit that, on this account, 'the whole fullness of deity' is not present in Jesus, as Colossians 2.9 claims that it is. Rather, 'Jesus lived out *as much* of the divine goodness, love, etc. as could be expressed in the thirty or so years of a particular human life in a particular time and place' (Hick, 1993, p. 76). This suggests that incarnation must involve some *qualification of divinity* in order to be an incarnation. But perhaps we really can't 'have everything' with God.

Second, we appear to have ended up with what is called a 'degree Christology', in which Jesus differs only in degree and not in kind from other religious figures – even if he expresses the love of God more than any other human being does. But Christian theology has normally wanted to affirm the *unique status of Jesus* as God's only Son, over against any potential rivals. There are an increasing number of Christians today, however, who question this absolutist theology of religions. And some go so far as to say that all major faiths are equally valid ways to experience the transcendent, and equally effective routes to salvation of some sort or another. And the philosopher of religion, John Hick, is one of their champions (see Hick, 1995; 2004, part 4). For Hick, Jesus was 'a Spirit-filled man . . . who was open to God's presence to a truly awesome extent and was sustained by an extraordinarily intense God-consciousness'; but he was only 'son of God' in 'the familiar metaphorical sense that was prevalent in the world of his time . . . indicating that he was close to God, open to God's presence, doing God's will' (1995, pp. 91–4).

Another general criticism of functional accounts of Christology is that function implies nature. Things and people can do what they do because of what they are; they have the sort of nature that enables them to perform this sort of function. Does this return us to a nature-Christology? Do we have to say what it is about the being of Jesus, perhaps about the nature of his mind, that allowed him truly to reveal and express God's truth, love and forgiveness? What might that be then? And does it make Christ *different* in his being from us: so different that he can also be God to us, while somehow remaining identical to us (one and the same as us)?

Interestingly, while later nature-Christology spoke of a full human nature being 'assumed, not absorbed' in the incarnation, it also insisted that the Word or Son of God was doing the assuming – taking over the humanity, directing it, being 'in charge' as it were, in the one (divine) person. Some would interpret this as a *qualification of the humanity* that imperils Christ's identity with us.

Other Christological issues

So far we have rather skated over the clauses of the creeds that affirm the pre-existence, the virgin birth – or, rather, virginal conception – and the ascension of Jesus. These three doctrines have been widely contested.

The language of descent from and ascent to heaven is obviously to be taken metaphorically: Jesus cannot literally come down from heaven or ascend back into it if heaven (or God) is not located within our physical world – even 'above the bright blue sky' – but is a different reality altogether, a transcendent one. Before we look more closely at the ascension, however, what of the '*descent*' of Christ 'to the dead' mentioned in the Apostles' Creed? This refers to the idea in 1 Peter (3.18b–20; 4.6) of Christ's redemptive visit in the spirit after his death to the shades of the disobedient (?) dead – signifying those who died before his incarnation, or even the rebellious angels. Later commentators, however, have some-times related this clause in the creed to the more this-worldly hell of Christ's life and death, or viewed it as part of his victory over hell. Calvin saw it as Christ's sharing of the experience of the con-demned sinner.

Christ's *ascendency*, the 'present lordship of the exalted Christ' (Cranfield, 2004, p. 45), was taken as read by the early Church. They worshipped him and prayed to him. But the *ascension*, under-stood in terms of the transition to this state, is only recorded by Luke (Luke 24.51; Acts 1.9). It is an event that is difficult to describe, except mythologically. Theologically, however, the ascension – and Jesus' departure from his disciples (John 16.7) – means that 'Jesus' significance is made universal, but still as the particular person that he is' (Gunton, 2002, p. 112). Understood in this way it offers a positive contribution to Christology.

But what about Jesus' *pre-existence* prior to his birth? The doctrine of the Trinity – which we shall eventually have to tackle – addresses this issue in a particular (though hardly simple) way. In doing so it develops certain New Testament claims, such as John 17.5 and Colossians 1.15–17, which may have originally been the equivalent of Jewish claims about the significance of – even a sort of personi-fication of – God's Law, Spirit and Word. Those who treat the New Testament language of pre-existence as wholly metaphorical some-times say that it expresses nothing more than the claim that Jesus was not an afterthought but that he was part of God's plan – 'in God's mind' – from the very beginning.

The *virgin birth* is another doctrinal stumbling block for many. It appears in the Gospels of Matthew and Luke but nowhere else in the Bible. Although it features in both creeds, many modern theologians contend that it 'does not belong at the centre of the gospel' (Küng, 1993, p. 44). In any case, it was a claim that was not wholly unusual in ancient times when speaking of great figures. Our present-day world view, however, is more suspicious of 'nature miracles' like this, if this is what it is. It also raises the theological question as to whether the virginity of Jesus' mother is compatible with his full humanity. And even those who are wedded to a nature-Christology must reckon with the fact that God's nature is essentially spiritual and bodiless. In which case we should not expect that in the conception of Jesus, God's being is necessarily *physically* related to, or replaces, the second set of chromosomes that a human father normally contributes in the fertilization of the mother's egg. Needless to say, that sort of scientific speculation was wholly alien to the thinking of the New Testament writers and the later fathers of the Church. So perhaps we shouldn't embark on it either.

TO DO

After all this, how do *you* respond to all these different ways of thinking about Jesus?

Hans Küng summarizes the 'original sense' of the incarnation of Jesus Christ along the following lines, which he describes as being unconcerned with metaphysical speculations about pre-existence (and, in this respect, like the first chapter of John's Gospel), and lying closer to Jewish and Jewish-Christian thought than to any 'Greek conceptual model of "incarnation"' – which in this context 'must to some degree be buried'.

Becoming man means that in this person God's word, will and love took on human form. In all his speaking and proclamation, in all his actions, in his fate, in his whole person, the man Jesus did not act as God's double ('a second God'). Rather, he proclaimed, manifested and revealed the word and will of the one God. . . . The one in whom, according to the witnesses, word and deed, teaching and life, being and action, fully coincide, is in human form God's word, God's will, God's image, God's Son. (Küng, 1993, pp. 60–1)

What do you think? Does this say enough to allow us to speak of 'a unity of Jesus with God'?

Further reading

Astley, J., 2010, *SCM Studyguide to Christian Doctrine*, London: SCM Press, Ch. 7.

Astley, J., Brown, D. and Loades, A. (eds), 2009, *Christology: Key Readings in Christian Thought*, London: SPCK.

Inbody, T., 2005, *The Faith of the Christian Church: An Introduction to Theology*, Grand Rapids, MI: Eerdmans, Ch. 8.

McGrath, A. E., 2007, *Christian Theology: An Introduction*, Oxford: Blackwell, Ch. 11.

McGrath, A. E., 2008, *Theology: The Basics*, Oxford: Blackwell, Ch. 4.

Stiver, D. R., 2009, *Life Together in the Way of Jesus Christ: An Introduction to Christian Theology*, Waco, TX: Baylor University Press, Ch. 7.

7

Creation:
Our Costly Earth

The topics in this chapter represent important and controversial areas of Christian belief. The creeds, however, pass over them either briefly or entirely.

Creation

We are told in both our creeds that God is the 'creator/maker of heaven and earth'. The Nicene Creed adds 'of all that is, seen and unseen', and later and mysteriously speaks of the only Son of God as one through whom 'all things were made' (cf. John 1.3; 1 Corinthians 8.6; Colossians 1.15–20; Hebrews 1.2–3). This motif perhaps points to the fact that creation is also 'a redemptive act', part of the same 'continuous process' (Lampe, 1977, p. 180).

TO DO

Read the following biblical passages, making a note of any themes that might contribute to a doctrine of creation and any problems to which the texts give rise.

Genesis 1.1—2.4a; 2.4b–25; Job 38.1–18; Psalms 104.14–30; Isaiah 40.25–31; 42.5–7; Romans 8.18–24.

If you took the trouble to wade through all this material you may have felt rather overwhelmed, and not just because of the number of verses! When the Bible speaks of God's creation it gives us poetry and hymns that stretch our imagination almost beyond its breaking point. It wants to overawe us.

But it mustn't extinguish our critical faculties. Richard Dawkins gets it right when, writing about the patient interrogation of nature by scientists, he comments on an aesthetic experience that is enriched and not reduced by a deeper study. 'The feeling of awed wonder that science can give us is one of the highest experiences of which the human psyche is capable. . . . It is truly one of the things that makes life worth living' (Dawkins, 1998, p. x). Now theist and atheist alike can agree about the wonder of the universe, although only the first will see it as *God's* wonder and therefore as a manifestation, channel and expression of God's gracious love; and as a sort of sacrament (see Chapter 3). Theological study may enhance the wonder that is associated with this 'extra dimension' that undergirds nature, just as the scientific study of nature enhances the wonder of nature itself.

What else might have struck you in these readings? The very existence of two different accounts of creation, written at very different times but sitting next to each other in the book of Genesis, should alert us to the dangers of taking religious poetry literally – and 'myth' too (in the neutral, technical sense of a story-metaphor). It is especially dangerous to read such material as if it represented a literal scientific account. The Genesis stories offer us something very different from the theories provided by the physicists and astronomers who study the origin of the physical universe, and the evolutionary biologists who trace the development of life – that emergent glory of the creation – and even speculate on its origins within nature. The Bible is not trying to 'do science', and neither are theology and the creeds.

Rather, these things add to and complement the scientific accounts of the world (which is the term that is still used to cover our whole vast universe), by exploring religious, theological and metaphysical explanations that speak of another reality. As this non-created reality lies behind and beyond the creation that exists in space and time, it is necessarily hidden from scientific study; nevertheless this is the reality in which all created things and their relations are grounded and on which they depend. It is, of course, God.

Theology does not contradict science, it supplements it. In effect, whenever we undertake an observation or any scientific study of nature this constant refrain whispers softly (or sings loudly) into our ears: '*and* the Lord has made it all, and sustains it in being by his love'.

That is the great *double entendre* of the doctrine of creation. For creation has two dimensions and two meanings:

- (not only) *the bringing of the universe into existence*, out of nothing, at the beginning of time (and hence 'before' the Big Bang), together with the laws of interaction of matter and energy that are implicit within its inner structure and which therefore lead to further change, including the emergence of complex entities that can make other entities;
- (but also – and, in fact, more significantly) *the keeping of the universe in existence*, through an incessant act of 'continuous creation'. For the universe *now* 'depends on a divine thread of preservation above the abyss of nothingness', into which it would fall if God withdrew the divine presence, power and grace (Brunner, 1952, p. 34). 'The world exists', Thomas Aquinas wrote, 'just so long as God wills it to' (*Summa of Theology*, 1a, question 46, 1).

The cost-benefit analysis

What's in creation for us though – and what's in it for God?

From our side:

- Clearly, we get *everything*. Creation is our generous God's great sacramental gift, without which we could not thrive because we would not exist at all.

- In the end, at the end and in its ultimate purpose, creation is good (Genesis 1.31), and 'good for us'. Unlike some religious and philosophical belief systems, Christianity does not view matter or the physical as intrinsically evil. Quite the opposite, in fact, for it comes from God's hand and God's 'signature' may be found within in (McGrath, 2008, p. 52); and we humans have been created-evolved as a part of it, in and towards God's image (Genesis 1.26–27).
- We get to exercise responsible stewardship for it, as we receive an ongoing trust from God over his gift of creation – the one gift that truly keeps on giving.
- It evokes in us a response of wonder, gratitude, reverence and delight.
- It is, however, a risky place, where we are liable to suffering and heading for death (see below).

From God's side:

- The creation is intended for God's delight also. As Jürgen Moltmann puts it, creation is 'for the sake of the sabbath', God's rest, the 'feast of creation's redemption' – which is creation's meaning and end (Moltmann, 1985, p. 277).
- God keeps us close, or else creation would cease to be. As creator, God must always be present to us and to all things that exist. It seems that God wishes to sustain this unconscious relationship of dependence for the sake of the possibility of a deeper relationship: our conscious, free response to God and God's love.
- But this benefit to us is costly for God. The risk God takes in creating at all is the danger of making another reality that is intended to become, at least partly and at some stage, independent of its creator. This is risky for God because it is at this stage that the creation may rebel – like children who know no better and adults who surely should. And what could happen has happened; the risk was and remains all too real. (Process thinkers argue that freedom – and therefore God's risk – extends throughout the universe.)

> **TO DO**
>
> Modelling God as a loving parent, ourselves as God's children and creation as (a much more radical type of) procreation may encourage us to develop the metaphor of God's parental relationship with us further. In what significant ways, then, is creation (a) like and (b) unlike the relationships that human parents have with their children?

Children, whether infant or adolescent (and sometimes when grown-up), can have a very superficial view of what is involved in being a parent. Most of us only really begin to understand – and certainly to feel – what this all about if we become parents ourselves. Asking a young child what they think their parents do all day, and why, can be a chastening exercise. It shows us how little they see of the wider picture.

What does God do all day?

In a debate in the House of Commons reported in Hansard (vol. 416, cc 14–5 §21, 5 January 2004), the Conservative MP for Chipping Barnet, Sir Sydney Chapman, asked, 'Can the Minister tell the House whether the Church insures its buildings against acts of God? [Laughter.] If it does, does that not show a certain lack of faith, and if it does not, does that not show a lack of acumen?' He received the reply that this was 'not a matter that would properly concern the Second Church Estates Commissioner'. Quite right too.

The phrase 'acts of God' appears to be going out of fashion in the insurance industry, although it is still enshrined in British law, where it defines events that are caused by nature rather than human agency and could not be prevented by any amount of control, care, foresight or planning. (The phrase has always sounded a little presumptuous to me, as it is mostly used to identify only accidental and harmful events and rather suggests that they are the consequences of divine whim.)

But theology takes a broader and more positive perspective on God's activity, as covering – well, nearly everything:

- initial creation;
- continuing preservation;
- general providential ordering and even 'steering' of nature, evolution and history within the limits of (God's) laws of nature;
- special (or particular) providential care: as above, but here expressed in unexpected events that benefit particular individuals or groups (many 'answers to prayer' fall into this category), yet which still have an ordinary scientific explanation;
- miracles – unusual and (currently) *scientifically inexplicable* events that bestow help where it is badly needed, and/or provoke religious awe.

By no means every Christian believer or theologian believes that God acts in every one of these ways. In particular, since the rise of modern science we have become much more sceptical of miracles. And liberal theology in general has tended to collapse the whole range of activity into the categories of God's creation and preservation of the universe, arguing one or more of the following points.

- 'All events alike are miracle' (Schleiermacher, 1958, p. 114) in the sense that they should all evoke our awe and gratitude.
- Providence (and even miracle) lie in the eye of the beholder, who should be willing to view all events as being – at some level, although often at some distance – willed or permitted by God. God is no more present and active in miracles than in the regular behaviour of the world that operates under the (God's) laws of nature.
- God would not 'intervene in' or 'suspend' the laws of a nature that God has already created and now sustains.
  However, the idea of *miracle as an intervention* rather suggests:
  (a) that God is an interfering God, but 'to interfere you have to be an alternative to, or alongside, what you are interfering with', and 'if God is the cause of everything, there is nothing that he is alongside' (McCabe, 1987, p. 6); and

(b) that nature is a closed, determined system, a clock-like machine; whereas modern science has shown it to be more open and unpredictable than that – 'a set of emergent, flexible and open systems . . . open to a purposive shaping'. 'Having its origin in God', nature is always 'orientated towards God', and God may take the elements of nature beyond their natural powers 'so as to show [their] supernatural origin, foundation and goal' (Ward, 1990, pp. 126, 179, 181; cf. Doctrine Commission of the Church of England, 2005, pp. 233–59).

- Even if God can and does perform miracles, why does he not do so more often – and to better effect?

TO DO

Do you expect, or pray for, miracles? Or for 'providential' acts, such as healings or good weather? What difference would (or did) it make to your prayers and expectations if (or when) you were convinced that God only acts 'according to the laws of nature'?

Whose act is it anyway?

A further issue here is that *our own actions* are our own responsibility, although God remains responsible for keeping us in existence. Additionally, God may be said to influence our actions as and when we respond to and cooperate with God's creative-sustaining-providential presence, and/or any additional, extraordinary operations of God's grace, to the extent that our actions may be said to be *both* our own *and* God's (cf. Ephesians 3.20; Philippians 2.13; Colossians 1.29).

While all theologians are keen to affirm all this, most of them insist that our actions are only truly our own – even if in the above sense they are also God's – if we have true freedom of the will, however limited that may be. Historically there has been intense theological debate over whether our actions would continue to be our responsibility if God were to 'foreordain' or 'predestine' them (as Calvin and others assert). In my view God would rob us of real freedom were he wholly to *determine* our behaviour in advance in this manner.

Why do we suffer?

If God can and does act towards creation in the ways listed above, why is there so much evil about? Does God do too little? Isn't God in control of everything? Are some of God's actions simply not good enough from our perspective – not fit for (our) purpose? Or doesn't God really care? These are some of the hardest questions Christian belief has to face. Many of its critics say that Christianity can only offer partial or inadequate answers (or, better, 'responses').

The credal affirmations that provide the setting for this '*problem of evil*'[1] – that is, the beliefs that ensure this is 'a problem' that requires an explanation – are represented by the claims that there is *one* God who is the *creator of all* there is, and who is both *almighty* and our *Father*. The raw material available in the creeds for responding to the problem of evil are its claims about a salvation that comes through Christ's incarnation, crucifixion and resurrection, his future role as judge and our future hope for resurrection, and the statement that God's kingdom 'will have no end' in 'the life of a world to come'. These credal affirmations are discussed in Chapters 5, 6 and 9.

Looking outside the creeds, however, Christian reflection has offered a range of responses to the intellectual or theological problem of evil that go well beyond this doctrinal material. It is likely that you will have reflections of your own to contribute.

---

1 The word 'evil' is used here to cover not only the wrongdoing of human (or supernatural) agents and the pain and suffering it causes ('moral evil') but also pain and suffering caused by physical events within Nature ('physical' or 'natural evil').

TO DO

If an agnostic or atheist friend, or a puzzled child, asked you why people suffer in God's world, how would you respond?

Easy answers to a hard problem?

Faced with what the novelist Muriel Spark branded 'the only problem', it is tempting for Christians to make their excuses too quickly.

They may contend that God is actually a *finite God*, limited in knowledge and power. Justin Martyr in the second century and 'process theologians' today have portrayed God as creating not from nothing but out of an already existing, recalcitrant ('obstinately disobedient') *chaos*. This independent factor would certainly limit God's ability to mould the universe entirely according to his heart's desire, leaving chaotic forces within the creation that may generate evil disorder. (Perhaps Genesis 1.2 might even suggest such a scenario.)

Christianity on the whole, however, has followed Irenaeus, another second-century theologian, by insisting on the more radical view of a creation 'out of nothing' (Latin, *ex nihilo*). Unlike humans, who can only 'create' out of material that already exists, God 'called into being the substance of his creation, when previously it had no existence' (Irenaeus, *Against the Heresies*, 2.10.4).

But if there is nothing from outside to limit God, is the explanation that God is simply not up to the job? Mainstream theology has insisted that the creator God is unlimited in power and knowledge. In other words, God:

- can do anything that can be done (is 'omnipotent');
- can know anything that can be known (is 'omniscient').

It is because of such powers that God is frequently declared to be unlimited, '*infinite*' (= not finite). In which case, whatever we might want to say, God cannot excuse Godself, in the ways that we can and do, by appealing to the inadequate materials we bought for that DIY job, or the dim students who turned up for our lectures (not you, of course). In the theology of creation, however, the buck always stops on *God's* desk.

What can we say, then, by way of mitigation, if God is supposed to be both so great and so good? In the landscape of *'theodicy'* (the defence of God's goodness and power in light of the existence of evil), two paths have been particularly well travelled.

An almighty God cannot prevent all evil

This cannot be because of any lack of power or knowledge; rather because God has chosen to create a *physical* universe containing physical creatures and not (or not only) a spiritual heaven made up of spiritual beings – that is, minds that do not occupy any space. Much suffering can be explained as 'an inevitable consequence of the sort of world in which [we] exist' (Ward, 1990, p. 55), for there are inevitable physical limits to a physical world and these inevitably give rise to pain and suffering in certain circumstances. Matter *does* occupy space, and pain is caused – in creatures that can feel it – when two physical objects come to occupy the same space at the same time, as when a cancerous growth presses on pain receptors. This 'mutual interference of systems', Austin Farrer contends, is 'the grand cause of physical evil'. So why does God not eliminate it?

> Poor, limping world, why does not your kind Creator pull the thorn out of your paw? But what sort of a thorn is this? And if it were pulled out, how much of the paw would remain? How much, indeed, of the creation? What would a physical universe be like, from which all interference of systems was eliminated?
>
> It would be no physical universe at all. . . . The physical universe could be delivered from the mutual interference of its constituent systems, only by being deprived of its physicality. (Farrer, 1966, pp. 50–1)

God chose, however, to create *embodied* creatures, and not only minds or spirits, such as angels. (And pain evolved because it mostly serves the good purpose of keeping organisms away from danger.)

An all-loving God would not want to prevent all evil

A universe that contains certain types of evil may in some ways be *better* than a universe without any evil. If so, God would have a 'morally sufficient reason' for allowing these evils. It is often said that God's power may be 'unfailing' and 'perfect', and yet that this power is not 'absolute or unqualified [because] it is determined and limited' by God's character. And God could not remain God and 'contradict his own character' (Cranfield, 2004, p. 15; cf. 2 Timothy 2.13). So what does God *will*?

The Free Will Defence argues that human sin is the risk that God takes in creating beings with real free will. But it is better that God should have created truly free and responsible beings who might do wrong, rather than programmed robots who could be guaranteed never to do wrong. And God could never really value our goodness or worship if we were causally determined automata, operating as mere extensions of the divine will.

Augustine broadened this defence to explain the pain and suffering caused by natural disasters and disease as well. He believed that all human beings inherited original guilt as a part of original sin from Adam (see Chapter 3), and therefore rightly suffer pain, suffering and death as God's punishment for *Adam's fall*, along with any punishment they justly suffer for their own sins. This theodicy has often been taken further, so as to cover a *fall of angelic beings* that occurred prior to the creation of humans, resulting in malevolent beings who inflict natural evil on our world. Michael Lloyd argues that such rebellious beings also distort nature's processes so that suffering becomes part of evolution, adding that humans were introduced to heal these wounds through their ruling of creation but instead 'they joined in that rebellion' (Lloyd, 2012, p. 86).

However, predation and pathogens will almost inevitably arise within a nature in which competition for food, mates and territory help to drive natural selection – which is itself an unavoidable process – and therefore evolution, and where death is a necessary condition for both (cf. Astley, 2009). Such evils represent the inevitable, self-inflicted 'collateral damage' of a material creation to which God has allowed the freedom to evolve in its own way, rather than a going wrong of a process created to be always wholly benign.

But there is another response that may be made within this section. John Keats applied the phrase the *Vale of Soul-Making* to our present world, preferring to think of it in this way rather than as 'a vale of tears'. This concept is a key element in an alternative explanation of the existence of evil in God's creation that does not depend on the concept of a fall. Briefly put, the argument holds that some natural evil is necessary if the world is to provide an environment in which free human beings may morally and spiritually develop. For without evil in our world, there could be no virtue, for fairly obvious reasons.

- Compassion, cooperation, courage and kindness, for example, can only develop where they are needed; that is, in a world that is capable of suffering and danger.
- If God always prevented the 'bad' consequences of our 'wrong' acts (the suffering that we cause by our sinning), we would never recognize the wrongness of our evil intentions and therefore never grow up morally.

In fact in a painless world:

The race would consist of feckless Adams and Eves, harmless and innocent, but devoid of positive character and without the dignity of real responsibilities, tasks, and achievements. By eliminating the problems and hardships of an objective environment, with its own laws, life would become like a reverie in which, delightfully but aimlessly, we should float and drift at ease. (Hick, 1985, p. 307)

We may regret that the world is such a testing and often dangerous place – but this is the only sort of environment that can produce
moral and spiritual growth. Additionally, this theodicy explains the
chance distribution of natural evils, for if suffering was always clearly
seen to be for our eventual good (as in this theodicy, or as a just
punishment for wrong acts, as Augustine thought), it might never
evoke our sympathy or caring help. But that effect is the whole
point of it (cf. Astley, 2007, Ch. 5).

This 'gratuitous' and therefore 'tragic' distribution of suffering
makes life harder, of course; for on this view the cry, 'Why me/Why
her?' can receive no better answer than, 'This stuff just happens' (in
a creation that is both physical *and* designed for moral growth). But
isn't this more plausible than the answer that everyone still seems to
expect – and which, I have to admit, is advocated in some parts of
the Bible – that '*Someone* must have sinned'? In any case, that was
the response pronounced by Job's comforters, who were criticized
by God (see Job 4.7–9; 8.4–6; 11.4–6; 21.29–30; 42.7), and the
theodicy that Jesus himself refuses to affirm (see Luke 13.1–5; John
9.1–3; cf. Matthew 5.45).

But many reject the implication that the risk of suffering was
always intended to be a constituent part of creation, insisting that
'suffering is never God's purpose . . . what He wants for any of His
creatures' (Lloyd, 2012, pp. 64–72). We need to make some sort
of distinction, however, between what God plans (and therefore
intends, or as some would say 'consents to') as a *means*, and the
bigger plan that God ultimately intends – and actually desires – as
an *end*, but which can only be gained through these means. In this
world, suffering is allowed as a real evil to be resisted because there
is no other way of developing the good character that results in
courageous, faithful and loving actions – which is what God really
intends – except by fighting and curing real human woes, ignorance and dangers. A life without any suffering sounds perfect. But
a 'heaven on earth' is no way for us to develop into the likeness of
God, as it means that no one will ever actually *need* our love.

A final response to evil also falls under this heading. It is that, like
the limited children we are, we simply cannot see God's greater

picture. Many regard *the future good of heaven* as something that will be so good that it will justify retrospectively all the evils that were a necessary means to this end (see Romans 8.18–23). Or it may be that our final *experience of God* at the last may 'engulf . . . even the horrendous evils humans experience in this present life here below', so that we shall then not doubt that our lives were 'worth living', despite everything (Marilyn McCord Adams, in Adams and Adams, 1990, p. 218).

But such experiences do not actually 'explain' evil. We know enough about growing up, however, to know that things appear and feel different when we look back. Perhaps our suffering, and the suffering of those we love, will somehow 'fall into place' eventually. Or they will lose their position of dominance in our concerns in some other way. Let us hope so.

TO DO

Which (combination?) of the various responses to the problem of evil seem to you to be (a) plausible, intellectually and theologically, and/or (b) spiritually helpful?

What do you make of the following claim: 'If beings like human persons are going to exist, they have to exist in a universe in which suffering and death are necessary' (Ward, 2008, p. 80)?

Further reading

Astley, J., 2010, *SCM Studyguide to Christian Doctrine*, London: SCM Press, Ch. 8.

Astley, J., Brown, D. and Loades, A. (eds), 2003, *Creation: A Reader*, London: T. & T. Clark, Ch. 1.

Astley, J., Brown, D. and Loades, A. (eds), 2004, *God in Action: A Reader*, London: T. & T. Clark, Chs 1 and 2.

Davis, S. T. (ed.), 2001, *Encountering Evil: Live Options in Theodicy*, Louisville, KY: Westminster John Knox Press, Introduction and Ch. 2.

Inbody, T., 2005, *The Faith of the Christian Church: An Introduction to Theology,* Grand Rapids, MI: Eerdmans, Ch. 6.

McGrath, A. E., 2007, *Christian Theology: An Introduction,* Oxford: Blackwell, pp. 216–35.

Ward, K., 2008, *The Big Questions in Science and Religion,* West Conshohocken, PA: Templeton Press.

8

Father God:
One Almighty Mystery?

And so – at long last, you may be thinking – we come to the doctrine of God. This looks like 'theology proper', as one meaning of that word is the study (*logos*) of God (*theos*). Obviously all doctrines and every part of the creeds are about God, and most academic theologians hold that Christian doctrines should hold together like an interconnected web, so that we can trace at least some implications and links of thought from each article of Christian belief to every other one. But now we *focus* on the question, 'Who, and what, is God?'

TO DO

What do you believe – *really* believe – about the nature of God? What sort of God do you believe in, and which portrayals of God do you passionately reject? Try to express *your* answers in a paragraph or two that capture your doctrine of God. Please be honest, but also aim to be clear and to think it through.

(As this exercise may be the most personal one in the book, don't feel that you have to share all your 'words about God' with anyone else, unless and until you are ready to.)

Talking mystery

In his introduction to Christian theology, *Faith Seeking Understanding*, Migliore begins his chapter on God with the following sentence: 'Christian theology begins, continues, and ends with the inexhaustible mystery of God.' That is a very good place to start. Readers who have taken that claim to heart may not be surprised to find that his next paragraph begins, 'Talk of God has become a problem for many people today' (Migliore, 2004, p. 64).

If God is a mystery, God-talk will always be a problem. David Cunningham's text, *These Three are One* (which is in no sense introductory!), describes the sort of God-talk that is appropriate to a God of mystery:

> [Christians] believe that God is ultimate mystery, and their language for God must be tentative and provisional if they wish to make good on that belief. . . . The congregation that allows a variety of different voices to speak different names for God is a congregation that is fully aware of this mystery. (Cunningham, 1998, p. 284)

And right at the end of his book, this author comments further on the 'uncertainty, tentativeness, and provisionality' that mark the theological task, writing:

> This does not mean that theologians can have nothing to say. . . . But theological claims and references do not yield absolute and unrevisable answers to our questions. Our rock, our certainty, is God – not the shifting sands of theological formulation. (p. 337)

An earlier scholar, Ian Ramsey (who became an Anglican bishop), in discussing what is disclosed in revelation and discerned in religious experience, emphasized that 'we can be sure about God; but we must be tentative in theology' (Ramsey, 1965, p. 89). 'Theological humility' is required here: what Ramsey elsewhere described as the 'theological stammering' and 'significant stuttering' of our human, limited, earthbound attempts to be articulate about a mystery.

So please don't beat yourself up if your little treatise on the nature of God seems to you – or others – slightly inadequate. Everyone's theology must appear inadequate from where God is looking.

A big part of the problem is that we only have human language to work with, because that is the only language that we can understand. We can, therefore, only speak of God – and God can only 'speak' to us – in limited, earthbound, human language. We may coin some philosophical terms that apply only, or at least literally, to God: terms such as 'uncreated', 'eternal' or 'triune' (Three-in-One). Or we can unearth the abstract features hidden within the logic of our language, so as to attribute various *functions* to God without shifting their meaning, so that we can speak of God as literally 'making' (= bringing something into existence?) or 'healing' (= making someone better?), for example.

But most of the time we are obliged to rely on analogies and metaphors. In *analogy* the meaning that the word has when it is applied to humans is stretched and qualified in order for it to apply to God (who, for example, 'lives', 'loves' and 'acts', but not in the ways that embodied, finite persons perform these acts). In the case of *metaphors* and myths (story-metaphors, you will recall from Chapter 7), our human language is applied figuratively to God, who is not literally (or even 'really') a 'father', 'mother', 'rock' or 'fortress', although these 'tropes' illuminate our understanding of the Almighty, both significantly and vividly.[1]

Going to the pictures

'The picture of God in the Hebrew Bible is very dynamic. Many of the images are anthropomorphic (i.e. projecting human features and characteristics onto God)' (Markham, 2008, pp. 58–9). So the biblical God has a face, eyes, ears, arms, a voice and so on; and

---

1 For a brief summary of how descriptive religious language can work, see Astley 2014, Ch. 7; for a longer discussion, see Astley, 2004, Chs 4 and 5.

God displays a range of very human emotions and often engages in markedly human activity.

Children used to be encouraged to draw pictures of God, if only to give their Sunday School teachers something to giggle over afterwards. But what were they expected to draw, exactly; what on earth – or elsewhere – *could* they 'picture'? Inevitably these younger theologians followed in the venerable tradition of the illuminated manuscripts, great religious paintings and stained-glass windows, by portraying an old man with a beard, frequently enthroned on a cloud. I don't think many of the adult artists who produced this religious art actually thought God looked like this, or that he could be really pictured at all. That the biblical authors also realized they were anthropomorphizing about God, and hardly ever intended their divine descriptions to be taken completely at face value, is supported from Scripture itself – which insists not only that 'no one shall see [God] and live' (Exodus 33.20), but even that 'No one has ever seen God' (John 1.18).

We should bear all this in mind when reading Genesis 32.24–30, Isaiah 6.1–5 and similar passages.

TO DO

What do you make of those two 'descriptions' of God; or of the 'pictures of divinity' contained in Genesis 18.1–16; Exodus 24.15–18; Ezekiel 1.26–28 and other passages in the Bible?

What are the most striking and effective portrayals of God you have come across (a) in hymns and prayers and (b) in artistic representations? How *should* we interpret such divine visions and descriptions?

'Theophanies' (visible manifestations of God) are actually quite rare in the Bible, where they are always shrouded in mystery. What is much more common is the employment of human – or, as theologians would say, 'personal' – language in writing of God's activity. Although the directors of medieval mystery plays seemed content to cast a human actor in the role of God, that does not mean they thought God shouted like he did – even if they were lucky enough to cast a Brian Blessed. It makes much more sense for us, and for the authors of Scripture, to interpret references to God walking in his garden or shutting the door of Noah's ark (Genesis 3.8; 7.16) as figures of speech that should be treated as metaphors or, at the very least, as incorporating the partial similarity of analogies. And the same goes for the innumerable other accounts of God speaking, calling, coming down, leading out, healing, punishing, rescuing, guarding and sending, and so on – and on. How else could we ever speak of God, except by using the language of *human* activity?

> The simplest defence of anthropomorphism in our language about God is that it is indispensable, and that its limitations are no greater than those which we take in our stride in any secular use of metaphor. But there is also a strong positive case to be made for its retention. Belief in God depends to a small extent on rational argument, and to a larger extent on our ability to frame images to capture, commemorate and convey our experiences of transcendence. (Caird, 1980, p. 176)

As human beings we cannot do without such human imagery. More abstract language, like much abstract art, just doesn't work in the same way – at least not within religion (see pp. 75–6).

But let us return to our first question, and try to explore who and what God is – or could possibly be.

The Who-God (of Christian devotion and response)

Why does God matter to us? Well, why does anything and anyone matter to us? Mattering matters because it is a response to our deepest sense of value. We hold some things, ideas and people 'in high esteem'; we 'value' them. The origin of the word 'worship' lies in the Old English word *weorthscipe*, which means the 'acknowledgement of worth'. *The* God will only become *our* God when we come to think of, and feel about, God in a certain way, as worthy of our worship: when we begin to ascribe supreme worth to this reality, this individual, this person. Martin Luther wisely commented that 'whatever your heart clings to and confides in, that is really your God' (*Large Catechism*, The First Commandment). And this is why it is the *character of God* that really matters to us. We cannot worship who or what we do not value. This appears to be a logical, or at least a psychological – and in one sense, therefore, a spiritual – truth.

God is portrayed in the Bible and Christian theology as an agent, a 'doer', an active reality – and thus as 'personal'. The point of Christology is not mainly to make high claims about Jesus. Its deeper and fuller purpose is to make high claims about God. Christology expresses the Christian conviction that 'God is love, and those who abide in love abide in God, and God abides in them' (1 John 4.16), that 'God is Christlike and in him is no un-Christlikeness at all' (Ramsey, 1969, p. 98).

So the so-called '*religious and moral attributes*' of God must be pre-eminent in theology. These include God's love, goodness and grace; and God's justice and mercy. And God's 'Fatherhood' too, which is not of course to be understood physically. God can be liter-ally neither male nor female, being – in the language of the Anglican Articles of Religion – 'without body, parts, or passions'. (Female imagery for God is also to be found in the Bible, for example at Deuteronomy 32.18; Isaiah 49.15; 66.13; Luke 13.20; John 3.6.)

All such attributes imply that God is a free, responsible centre of experience, activity and response. Much more like a person than a stone, then; or even a fire.

TO DO

Try to make the longest list you can of the nouns and verbs applied to God in Scripture, using any help you can muster from concordances, works of theology and/or Internet searches. Then mark your list to indicate the use of personal or imper-sonal language, and (within the former category) masculine or feminine, and male or female vocabulary. Search out any modern hymns or prayers that use images for God that are not reflected in your list of biblical vocabulary.

Go through this list, asking yourself which aspects of this language about God we should treat positively and which negatively; that is, in what respects is God (a) like and (b) unlike an enthroned king, a fire or a wrestler and so on?

Which of these terms do you prefer to use in describing or worshipping God, and why?

Religious language tends to give us meaning with one hand while taking some of it away with the other. God is 'like this' (as in Jesus' parables, which often begin 'the kingdom of God/heaven is like . . . '); but God is always also 'unlike this' too. God is like a father in giving, keeping and caring for our life; but unlike a father in not being male (or bald, grumpy, an embarrassing dancer and so on). God's character and actions are like those of the most caring, forgiving, loving, active and alive person you have ever known. But God is still always going to be unlike her or him, in that God is not a finite person with their in-built or learnt characteristics. Their features include, naturally, their limited character and activities, especially in comparison with God's core property of self-giving, *unrestricted* love. God is always more than us, not less. Certainly, God is not limited by selfishness and sin.

Hence we sometimes feel we have to add something in order to stretch the meaning of our religious language further and push it out towards God. In particular we add qualifiers of exceeding or transcending, and speak of God not just as our father but as our 'heavenly' Father (or Mother). God is also 'infinitely' loving, 'wholly' just or the truly 'holy' one who exceeds all holiness.

This language encourages us to avoid all those lesser, imitation gods. In these ways God is unquestionably other than us, 'beyond' us, different from us. We must only worship the exceeding God.

The What-God (of theological reflection)

In the last section we were concerned with God as a personal God in relationship and therefore with *who* God is, in relation to us and the rest of the creation. In the topics we review in this section, theology employs impersonal, abstract and often technical language to answer a different question, '*What* is God?' or (more accurately), 'What is God *in Godself*?' Accounts of this What-God often employ philosophical, metaphysical language. Enveloped in this idiom, God has come to be understood as an absolute or ultimate, infinite and self-existent (uncaused), eternal and even immutable (unchanging) reality. These elements of God's nature have been called God's '*metaphysical attributes*', and they are used in an attempt to go more deeply into the inner structure of the being of God.

Whereas the religious and moral attributes of God derive from the Bible, and from Christian worship, piety and spirituality, the attributes we are concerned with here mostly came to the fore when Christianity engaged with Greek philosophy in the patristic and medieval periods, particularly through thinkers who drew on the thought of Plato and Aristotle. But similar reinterpretations have continued into modern times under the influence of very different philosophical views, including the process philosophy of A. N. Whitehead.

God's metaphysical attributes may seem remote from – and sometimes even incompatible with – the personal 'God of Abraham . . . Isaac, and . . . Jacob' (cf. Exodus 3.15), or the Father of Jesus (cf. Mark 14.36). But we should not be too ready to dismiss them, for a complete description even of ourselves must include impersonal data about our anatomy, biochemistry and economic value, alongside the more personal details of our character and relationships that may be provided by our parents, lovers, children or friends. Many of us have reason to be thankful that our bank balance and body-mass index are of less interest to our friends than these more personal and occasionally positive elements of our existence. But all the same, the impersonal data are also part of what makes us what we are. Even the material and materialistic dimensions of my existence (e.g.

being overweight or overdrawn) are truths about me, and in the end my matter and these matters matter as well (sorry!), especially when they impact on my personal being and relationships.

But enough about us – what of God? That God is a – or rather the – *spiritual being* underlies all attempts to understand God's true nature. 'God is spirit' (John 4.24). God is only personal in the form of a mind without a body (and therefore *invisible*), for God is 'bodiless' or *non-corporeal* – although capable of being embodied in Christ. While some have treated the creation as 'God's body', since God is essentially a spiritual being, God *requires* no body through which to act or communicate. Nor is God in Godself, as infinite spirit (and therefore as an 'unlimited person'), constrained in other ways by any physical body. God transcends all such material limitations.

Transcendent and immanent

The key metaphysical attribute of God is surely this *transcendence*. To transcend something is to go beyond it. Almost by definition, God ('The Transcendent') lies beyond the grasp of our human experience and language; and God's reality is a reality that goes beyond, or exceeds, any other (and therefore created) being, even human beings. God's *holiness* has been expressed as God's 'utter difference and distinction from all other beings' (Gunton, 2002, p. 55), and the claim is often heard that the otherness of God implies that God is utterly different from nature and even from us.

But 'utterly' is perhaps too strong a word. For if God were wholly different from us we could apply no human language to God at all. 'Exceedingly' may be a better adverb for indicating that God is 'extremely' and 'to a great extent', rather than wholly ('entirely', 'fully') or utterly ('completely', 'absolutely') different. A *wholly other* God would be wholly indescribable, which would deny theology even the weak whisper of a voice that religion usually permits it. *All* would be mystery. God must ever remain, however, beyond 'all we can . . . imagine' (Ephesians 3.20); but never wholly beyond.

God's attribute of transcendence does not conflict with our belief in God's presence alongside or even within all things, something that is technically expressed by the property of *immanence*. Indeed, God's otherness (transcendence, difference) and God's closeness (immanence, within-ness) both follow from God being the creator: the only non-created, independent reality, who both makes all other things from nothing and keeps all matter, energy and other minds in existence through the divine sustaining power. So the Creator God is both 'most high over all the earth . . . exalted far above all gods' (Psalms 97.9), *and also* 'nearer to us than we are to ourselves' (Barth, 1966, p. 38).

TO DO

Transcendence has an obvious connection with the idea of *mystery*.

> Conceptually, mystery refers to something we cannot get our minds around, cannot manage to grasp. . . . In face of mystery we face utter bafflement. Our response is not as much a matter of knowledge as it is of acknowledgment. (Inbody, 2005, p. 82)

The author uses the 'u'-word here. Does this take the idea of divine mystery too far? Or do we not take God's mystery seriously enough?

As I argued above, it is perfectly proper to say that God transcends us in God's personal attributes also, in God's character and relationships, such as love, mercy and justice, and as Infinite Father, Mother, Healer, Redeemer, Guide, Enabler, Maker and Friend. The difference that God makes to our lives, emotions and thoughts is very largely the result of this sort of difference. This is the exceeding-ness of God's transcendent love and of God's exceeding grace, and of the divine forgiveness that is beyond all human forgiving. This form of exceeding greatly matters to us.

God unlimited

But the transcendence of God's *being* also makes a spiritual differ-ence to us, in the attitudes we bring to our faith, our love and our hope. Thus God's ever-present-ness, or *omnipresence*, means that God may act and be known everywhere; that there is no 'where' beyond the reach of God's grace. And God's *omniscience*, *omnipo-tence* (see p. 95) and eternity allow us to trust more radically and hope more hopefully than we could ever do if God's knowledge and might were finite, or available only 'for a time' and not for ever.

The concept of God's *eternity*, however, is ambiguous. In much religious discourse it means everlasting existence – being without beginning or end, and therefore immortal. But that is still an exis-tence 'in time'. When time is applied to God, we may think of God existing in a different sort of time from our own, 'in God's time' if you like. Many theologians, however, have interpreted eternity as meaning 'outside all time', 'time*less*'. If God were outside time it might be possible for God to know our past, present and even future timelessly. God would then be like a fell walker looking down at a road in the valley below and seeing it all in one glance – seeing where these less adventurous ramblers have walked and have yet to walk, as well as where they are presently walking. This account might mean that God can know what we are going to do in the future, even though our acts remain (partly) free and therefore (partly) unpredictable. (Note that this is very different from the idea of God's predestination of our future actions – see pp. 93–4.)

But timelessness would also mean that any verbs we apply to God must carry a *very* different meaning than they do in our own case. The question is whether that difference is just too different. What could it mean, on this view, to say that the (timeless) God *acts*; or that such a God loves, saves, sustains or otherwise interacts with creatures that are themselves in time? How could that activity be conceived? Classical theology has often affirmed that God is also *immutable*, unchanging in being (and not just in intention or character). Many now believe that this way of thinking, which is derived from Greek philosophy rather than biblical revelation, raises the same problems. How could an immutable God also be 'personal', or act, or suffer in Christ?

TO DO

It is easy enough to find biblical texts to illustrate God's personal attributes. (Or wasn't it?) But God's metaphysical attributes are also suggested in Scripture. What links to these more abstract qualities can you find in the passages listed here?

Psalms 90.1–6; 97.9; 113.4–6; 139.1–12; Isaiah 40.25–31; 57.15; Mark 10.27; Acts 17.23–28; Romans 1.20; 8.38–39; Ephesians 1.17–19; 1 Timothy 1.17; James 1.17; 1 Peter 5.11; Revelation 4.8.

Do any other passages occur to you that express these, or other, themes about God's impersonal being? You may want to extend your search beyond the Bible and explore the language of Christian hymns and songs, prayers or liturgies as well.

The strong name of the Trinity?

In those churches that celebrate Trinity Sunday (which falls on the first Sunday after Pentecost for Catholics and Anglicans), there is frequently trepidation among the preachers and not a little weariness within their congregations. But everyone's spirits rise when we stand to sing 'St Patrick's Breastplate', C. F. Alexander's grand Victorian hymn loosely based on an early (likely eighth-century) Irish prayer for protection. It begins and ends by invoking the Trinity:

I bind unto myself today
The strong Name of the Trinity,
By invocation of the same,
The Three in One, and One in Three.

But what is that all about? And why does the Christian Church make such a fuss about what to most people outside and many inside its walls appears to be an obscure – if not self-contradictory – abstract formula?

TO DO

Riffle through the blessings, prayers and sentences from Scripture that are contained in your own church's prayer book, hymn book or orders of service; or listen to the spoken prayers used there. Listen or look out for any 'trinitarian formulae' that are used to invoke or refer to God, and list as many examples as you can find.

What do these phrases *add* to Christian prayer and worship, in comparison with the simple use of the word 'God'?

The Bible offers only the beginnings of a trinitarian view of God in its references to God, Christ and the Spirit as agents of salvation (and often creation too), and also in those passages that speak of the relationships between Jesus as Son and his Father and the relationships between the exalted Christ, the Holy Spirit and God the Father. But these references were enough to kick-start the development of trinitarian doctrinal thinking as early as the second century, in the context of the Church's debate over the person of Christ. The Apostles' Creed, which probably originated during this period in Rome, only hints at the Trinity in its threefold subject heading of Father, Son and Holy Spirit. The later formulation of the Nicene Creed, however, provides a more detailed description of the nature of 'the only Son of God' that identifies him with the Father; and it adds that the Holy Spirit 'proceeds from the Father' and 'is worshipped and glorified' with both Father and Son, and is therefore God as well.

Beyond the creeds, Christian theology came to speak of 'three persons' of 'one substance' – claiming that Father, Son and Spirit were three particular individual instances of the same universal essence or substance, something that we might call 'God-ness'. 'We may not know what divine essence is, but we know that the Father and the Son share the same essence or life', and the Spirit also (McIntosh, 2008, p. 123).

Trinitarian typology

Most Christians officially tick the trinitarian box, or as a minimum they sing about binding themselves to the strong name of the Trinity. While there have been a variety of ways in which this doctrine has developed, however, it cannot honestly be claimed that any of them figure strongly in the beliefs and spirituality of most ordinary Christians today, despite the current emphasis of much theological scholarship on the topic.

In its older formulation, trinitarian doctrine held that God is essentially one but becomes three as God reveals Godself *successively* through Christ and the Spirit, which are both God-as-God-appears-to-us. This view is labelled the '*Economic Trinity*', in contrast to the later affirmation of an 'Immanent' or '*Essential Trinity*' in which God is eternally and *intrinsically* three ('co-eternal') equal ('co-equal') persons. On this second view, what Christ and the Spirit reveal is God as God is in Godself, as a genuine threefold but interrelated Godhead – with the one God 'generating' (not creating), communicating, giving and loving *within* this unity, as part of God's inner life. Here 'God is communion', and therefore 'love is fundamental to his being, not an addition to it' (Zizioulas, 2008, p. 53).

No one pretends that these are easy concepts. But whatever God is, God must be a *mystery* that transcends human thoughts. Anyone who tries to get their head around the accounts modern physics gives of the nature of the simplest particles of matter will quickly realize that the building blocks of the world are themselves literally unimaginable, and all the old, comfortable, concrete images of the structure of the atom have now been – and have had to be – replaced by abstract mathematics. Perhaps we should not expect the inner nature of God the Infinite Creator to be any easier on the mind than the smallest part of God's finite creation.

So even advanced thinking about trinitarian theology has come to rely on analogies that *are* imaginable – but remain merely analogies, even mythologies. Historically, the Greek-speaking and Greek-thinking theologians of Eastern Christianity have preferred a very picturable *social analogy of the Trinity*, which likens it to three people in a close, mutual, loving fellowship – in which 'divine identity is essentially constituted as a constant ("faithful") interrelationship' (White, 2002, p. 30). The famous fifteenth-century Russian icon by Andrei Rublev, illustrating Genesis 18, pictures this.

TO DO

Try to find as wide a range as possible of visual pictures and symbols of the Trinity in the fabric and furnishings of the churches in your locality. A wider trawl with the help of library books and Internet search engines should produce many more – including the Rublev icon.

Which of these pictures of the Trinity 'work' for you, and why?

In Latin-speaking Western Christianity, the stress has been placed, at least historically, more on the oneness than on the threeness of God. Some of the 'symbols' of the Trinity that you may have viewed in the last exercise look like attempts to 'picture' this more monistic (one-istic) interpretation of a God who is one, despite the threeness.

Augustine offered a *psychological analogy of the Trinity* that appealed to three interrelated parts of one human mind: memory, understanding and will (or love). Later, other theologians wrote of three 'modes of being in God' rather than three persons. It must be remembered, however, that 'Person' is a technical term in the doctrine of the Trinity, where it was first used to denote concrete, individual identities – not human-type agents. Despite this, the social analogy, which is increasingly popular in academic theology, tends to use the word in a way that is much closer to our modern sense. That sort of person is, after all, eminently imaginable.

Augustine expressed unease with the language of persons in his great treatise on the Trinity, declaring that the term should really only be used so that we are not 'reduced to silence' on the subject of the divine mystery. And frankly, I'm with Augustine on this one.

Trinity for dummies?

Something closer to the Economic Trinity may be more useful within Christian teaching and practice. It is easier, more relevant and always necessary for Christians to affirm a threefold *experience* and *revelation* of God, which corresponds with God's threefold activity as creator, redeemer and sanctifier. Of course, we must think of the same God doing all these things and being known in all these ways. But our theological language goes with the functions and the experiences/revelations, and we tend to allocate different terms from our theological vocabulary primarily – but not exclusively – into three separate lists to convey the meaning and direction of travel of these three elements. So we speak of:

- God as '*father*' or 'creator', *creating* and sustaining our and God's *world*;
- God as 'word', '*son*' or 'saviour', *redeeming* us in and through our and God's *Jesus*;
- God as 'wind', 'breath' or '*spirit*', forming and *sanctifying* us in and through our and God's *Church*.

(But spirit and word can also be used when speaking of creation; the spirit of redemption; and Christ the saviour of the Church.)

These terms all mean different things, in that they have different connotations, but *ultimately* they all point to, refer to, denote the same God, who comes to us in three different ways and may be approached along three different paths. It might even be said that we see God in three different ways, from three different directions, which gives us different experiences and disclosures of one and the same God.

The world, Jesus and the Church are three separate but related theological topics. They are also three different media of revelation and three foci of religious piety and experience, and three places where God is active and may be found – as a loving father, a revealing-redeeming word and a storm-force breath of life. These three topics, media, foci, places and activities all overlap and interact, as we have seen in Chapters 2 and 5; but their fundamental unity is assured, as it is grounded in the one God.

We can conceptually abstract out and distinguish, within this one God's relationship with us, God's work of creation, redemption or sanctification. There is *some* succession in these activities, although they are all just elements within the one (but 'threefold') divine relationship and activity. All our experiences and responses happen in time and have historically occurred in succession; but it is always the same God who comes to us each time, and in every place and context. So we know that these abstractions, like our partial perceptions, must all really be capable of being unified. If there is only one God, then all these 'threes' must be somehow united. They must be one.

The mystery of God will inevitably baffle us as we seek to penetrate more deeply into it. And there are always going to be limits to how much we can know and say of God. (And the 'dummy' who writes this *does* recognize its theological inadequacy.) But whatever we believe, and however we express it, we must not let go of the fundamental belief that rests at the heart of Christ's gospel and gives our theology what life and warmth it has: that 'God is the mystery who is *for us*' (Norris, 1979, p. 49; cf. above p. 69).

So how do *you* understand God the Holy Trinity?

Further reading

Astley, J., 2010, *SCM Studyguide to Christian Doctrine*, London: SCM Press, Ch. 9.
Del Colle, R., 1997, 'The Triune God', in C. Gunton (ed.), *The Cambridge Companion to Christian Doctrine*, Cambridge: Cambridge University Press, pp. 121–40.

Doctrine Commission of the Church of England, 2005, *Contemporary Doctrine Classics*, London: Church House Publishing, pp. 3–272.

McGrath, A. E., 2007, *Christian Theology: An Introduction*, Oxford: Blackwell, Chs 9 and 10.

McGrath, A. E., 2008, *Theology: The Basics*, Oxford: Blackwell, Chs 2 and 6.

Ward, K., 2002, *God: A Guide for the Perplexed*, Oxford: Oneworld.

9

Resurrection:
Christian Hope and Eternal Life

And so we conclude our journey. 'At last', appropriately enough: for we do so with some reflections on our *end* – that is, our conclusion, our ultimate goal, and our deepest hope (or fear?). Where does it all lead, then; and what may we (all?) hope for?

'Eschatology' is the part of Christian doctrine that deals with such matters. The word comes from the Greek for 'the last things', which are traditionally listed as death, judgement, heaven and hell. More generally, eschatology covers the faith, longing and expectation that we – and history, and even life and nature perhaps – are 'going somewhere under the guidance of God', heading 'towards God's new world of justice, healing and hope' (Wright, 2007, p. 134). This is a dominant theme in the teaching of Jesus and the early Church, but it is also found throughout the Old Testament, in which the word of the LORD – given voice to by the prophets – not only threatened God's judgement on faithless Israel (e.g. Hosea 5.8–15; Amos 2.6–16) but also promised hope for the future for those who repented (e.g. Hosea 6.1–3; Amos 5.14–15).

> ## TO DO
>
> Read the following passages and reflect on the hoped-for future they express. Which of these elements, if any, form part of *your* Christian hope?

Isaiah 11.6–9; 40.1–11; 49.8–11; 54.9–14; 60.1–7; 61.1–4; 65.17–25; Amos 9.11–15; Matthew 24.29–51; 25.31–46; 1 Corinthians 15.35–57; 1 Thessalonians 4.13–18; Revelation 21.1–8, 22–27.

Too much, already? An understandable reaction, because this is very heavy theology – powerful, challenging and fervent. The imagery of hope in these texts can be daunting and disturbing but it can also address our deepest desires. In Hebrew Scripture the prophetic word speaks only of a *historical hope* for a restoration of Israel as she should be, since during most of the Old Testament period there was little expectation of a life beyond death, other than a shadowy half-existence in *Sheol* away from the presence of God (cf. Psalms 88.1–12; Isaiah 38.18). Yet even so, the hoped-for future is for a renewed, transformed world that transcends life and history as we now know it.

Later, the nature of this longing changes and the language became more 'apocalyptic', as hope is expressed in terms of visions of God's vindication of Israel and of judgement on her oppressors. These images were of something that was very much more 'out of this world' (see the Book of Daniel, for example). The apocalyptic tradition of eschatology is to be found in the New Testament too, expressing Jesus' own *transcendent hope* and that of the early Church. Both expected a more complete overturning of history, a bringing in of the kingdom of God 'with power'. Over time this came to be expressed in terms of a reign of Christ on earth before the final end of history and of the world, and a general resurrection of the dead and their final judgement by God.

Part of the impulse behind both the historical and the more transcendent forms of eschatology was the increasingly potent expectation of a reversal of the injustices of the world, in favour of a moral and spiritual rebalancing of virtue and vice with rewards and punishments. How can it be, people thought, that God's faithful are martyred, the innocent suffer and the poor widow and orphan are oppressed? Well, just you wait – eventually God will come in vindi-cation, to right all wrongs. So be warned, and be prepared.

Christian hope appears to be fundamental to Christian belief. In Christianity, 'belief in the resurrection is not an addition to belief in God but a radicalization of belief in God. It is a belief in God who does not stop half-way, but continues consistently right to the end' (Küng, 1993, p. 117).

Life beyond death?

Hope for a historical fulfilment within this life (or at least within our children's lives), as the right end to our present woes, raises no intellectual problems beyond theological issues concerning God's sustaining, providential or miraculous activity within this world. However, the more transcendent eschatologies that express a hope for a life *beyond* death, and a world beyond this world, clearly raise additional – and broadly philosophical – difficulties.

Some maintain that the very phrase 'life after death' is a contra-diction in terms. Whatever else a life beyond the grave could be, it must be *different* from this life (and to that extent, *mysterious*). And yet it must show continuity. There must be something that could enable us, and probably others as well, to identify this new life as belonging to the 'same person' as the one who once lived and sub-sequently died. Memory would serve for us, but there must be other criteria if we are to be identified by others: our reports of personal memories that we shared with them, perhaps, or the continuity of our character, or even a similar body.

But these are still only tests – evidence for the truth of our being the same person after death. Memory, body or character do not *constitute* our being the same person. For that, I must be the same centre of experience and action that I was before, the same 'self'. Perhaps only a creator God could ensure that, so that my 'personal identity' is guaranteed across the gulf of death by God recreating me or ensuring my continuing survival.

Resurrected life

This option takes death very seriously, recognizing that everything dies and that there is nothing naturally immortal about us. So God will have to act again, to make us again, if we are to live again. But God is, after all, the creator, so God can then be our re-creator if that is required.

When belief in an afterlife first developed in Hebrew thinking alongside a belief in a judgement to restore the moral balance, it was a time of intense oppression and bloody martyrdom in which a new act of God was felt to be greatly 'required'. This new hope took the form of a belief in *resurrection*. There is evidence for this only in a few, very late Old Testament texts, such as Daniel 12.1–3. However, this understanding became widely held by New Testament times. Jesus' own resurrection, though it is described as being (more or less) physical and happening on this earth, was still clearly understood as a resurrection to a new resurrected life, not a temporary resuscitation of someone who would die once again. So Jesus' resurrection became seen as the 'first fruits', the beginning and guarantee of the general resurrection that was to come (1 Corinthians 15.20, 23).

Resurrection is also the form of life after death that the creeds speak of, as 'the resurrection of the body' (Apostles' Creed) or 'the resurrection of the dead' (Nicene Creed). This second phrase better captures the notion of human beings as wholly mortal, and as a unity compounded of body and mind (or soul/spirit/self), rather than as a loose mixture of separable elements where the mind is capable of an independent, continuing existence as an *immortal soul*. On the first view, what I essentially am is an embodied mind who hopes for re-embodiment of some kind. On the second, I am essentially a disembodied soul who yearns to escape from the physical entombment of both my body and the world.

When Paul writes of our future 'spiritual' body (1 Corinthians 15.35–44, 50–57), he means a new, non-corruptible body animated by God's Spirit, which would be a transformation (or, better, re-creation) of our present body and mind *together*. But this is still a hope for a (broadly) physical, 'bodily' or 'corporeal' existence that reflects what we are now, but comes to exist in another physical reality. In contemporary terms, we may think of this resurrection world as an alternative universe occupying a different space and time from this one, or as a transformed version of our present world. In either case, the new world would be 'an actual world which will resemble our world of space, time and matter in all sorts of ways, even as it will be far more glorious' (Wright, 2006, p. 74). This resurrection is 'God's transforming completion, through his Spirit, of human life in the body', not a 'taking away of the human soul out of the world' (Gunton, 2002, pp. 152–3). However we think of it, though, it will be different from this life.

So even this resurrection option raises questions about identification and identity, particularly for a 'social heaven' (see below). Will your resurrected body be sufficiently similar to the body you had during life for your loved ones to identify you as the same person? But what about Granny who died when you were only six; how could she recognize you? And do we really want our bodies to be just the same as they were in life? After all, they have just failed to work, which is why we are dead. And what about disabilities, physical and mental (including dementia)? Our bodies and minds must be transformed enough to provide a new and *worthwhile*, pain-free and disease-free existence, but not so changed that we are unrecognizable to others. Or could that recognition be ensured in some other way?

The imagery of resurrection makes life after death imaginable, but the more imaginable it is the more puzzles arise. It is tempting, therefore, to play the mystery card, which surely should be ready in our hands to play at some point (many points?) in the discussions within this chapter. We mustn't take any of these descriptions of life after death too literally. 'What we will be has not yet been revealed' (1 John 3.2).

Disembodied life

The alternative, Platonic idea of a person as essentially being an immortal soul only temporarily trapped within a body was common in Hellenistic (Greek) culture. It came to influence Christian thinking strongly in later centuries, and has become the official doctrine of Catholic Christianity: 'every spiritual soul is created . . . immortal: it does not perish when it separates from the body at death, and will be reunited with the body at the final Resurrection' (*Catechism of the Catholic Church*, 2000, § 366).

Oscar Cullmann argued that the idea of natural immortality was an alien Greek import into Christianity, by contrast with the genuinely Christian doctrine of a resurrection that is dependent on God's gracious supernatural activity in a new act of creation (Cullmann, 1958). But a full doctrine of creation would have to recognize that God's activity is needed for *any* existence of the human (mind or) soul, even it is continuing in a disembodied form. In Christian theology, 'natural' always means created, and our afterlife remains dependent on God's continuing act of preservation of something. Disembodied survival might even require an additional miraculous act of God to keep the soul in existence, or to re-create it after death, which would bring the two understandings of resurrection and immortality closer together theologically – although they remain very different philosophical views (in terms of our human nature before, as well as after, death).

Both views speak of mystery. A life without a body would be even more changed from our present existence. Identification – and personal identity – can no longer depend on our having the 'same' body; and our experience and agency would have to be very different if we no longer had sense organs, limbs or lips through which to see, hear, act and express ourselves. But it is possible to imagine such a life based on our present experience of dreaming, in which we 'experience' and 'act' in a dream-world through a dream-body, which are entities created out of mental images rather than matter (cf. Price, 1965). Perhaps God could create such a dream after our death, giving all of us images of the same 'world' (and therefore one common dream) and allowing telepathic communication between souls, who might 'appear' in our dream-world clothed in bodies we could identify. This would give the hypothesis of a disembodied afterlife more plausibility (and as there would be no 'waking up' back into a physical world, this afterlife dream would be our only reality).

In fact the Christian tradition welded the idea of a disembodied soul on to the more biblical view of resurrection, treating the survival of our soul as an *interim state* between our individual death and the general (bodily) resurrection at the last judgement. It is at that stage that we would be 'reunited' with our bodies or, rather, God would create new bodies for us. Some contend that an interim state is implied by certain biblical texts (e.g. Luke 23.43; 1 Thessalonians 4.14). While often presented as a state of 'sleep', 'waiting' or 'rest', the idea also allows for further salvific activity. In traditional Catholicism this is reserved for those who are saved but 'imperfectly purified', through the cleansing of *purgatory*. That concept is mostly rejected by Protestants (and the Eastern Orthodox), but in some quarters the idea has been developed into an additional period of spiritual change and repentance, either in a disembodied or an embodied existence (see below).

TO DO

Explore the prayers, liturgies and hymns used in your own church at funerals or other services 'for the dead'. Try to tease out the underlying beliefs that they imply about the nature of life after death, God's judgement and our possible final destination.

Which themes resonate most strongly with your own beliefs and hopes, and with which do you feel uneasy, and why?

Judgement, heaven, hell

Both of our creeds confess belief in a judgement (of 'the living and the dead'). This is associated with the risen, ascended, glorified Christ, who bears the authority of God the Father (for he is seated at God's 'right hand'). Christ's *parousia* ('arrival', 'presence'), known also as his Second Coming (the incarnation being his first), is a coming-in-judgement. Yet it is longed for by the Church, as testified by many of our advent hymns and services, along with the plea at the end of the book of Revelation: 'Come, Lord Jesus!' (22.20).

Yearning for judgement seems an odd thing to do. But two aspects must be borne in mind.

- Throughout the Bible, 'the judgement of God is not a judicial enquiry or pronouncement but an *act* – the *doing* of justice, the righting of wrong', so 'what is being asserted is faith in the ultimate supremacy of good over evil' (Burnaby, 1959, p. 183). Judgement is the inevitable corollary of our freedom to respond positively or negatively to God and neighbour, to be 'for' Love or 'against' it. Christians are taught to pray 'your kingdom come, your will be done, on earth as it is in heaven'. When God's reign is finally realized, and God's salvation fully come, whatever resists God's will for good must somehow be fully overcome.
- But this should not to be thought of as a species of retribution or revenge, meted out by a distant, uncaring, destroying power. The Christian God is no despot. Indeed, it is *Christ* who comes as judge: the same Christ who came first 'for us and for our salvation', and who came to offer life, to heal and forgive and to raise us up and bring us God's blessing. 'The one through whom God's justice will sweep the world is not a hard-hearted, arrogant or vengeful tyrant, but . . . the Jesus who loved sinners and died for them' (Wright, 2007, p. 154). 'The God who is decisively revealed in the cross of Christ does not exercise vindictive judgment', but 'a loving judgment and a judging love that we know in the cross of Christ to be for our salvation rather than our destruction' (Migliore, 2004, p. 345).

As it is Christ who is to be the Judge, 'our whole conception of that judgement must conform itself to what we know of Christ'.

Judgement is coming, but this judgement cannot now be thought of as a rendering to all 'according to their works'.

> The judgement of God is the offer of forgiveness to sinners, and to stand before the judgement-seat of Christ can be nothing else but to be confronted as a sinner with the awful holiness of the love of God. On the issue of that dread confrontation the Creed is properly silent. But the question to all must be the same. 'Do you plead guilty or not guilty? Are you ready to be judged according to your deeds, or will you see yourself as you are, see yourself as God sees you – and pass through the consuming fire of God's forgiveness?' (Burnaby, 1959, p. 185)

This claim would put into a wider context the texts in the New Testament, *both* (a) those in which judgement is presented as being 'for what has been done in the body, whether good or evil' (2 Corinthians 5.10; cf. Matthew 7.21; 25.31–46; Revelation 20.12), *and* (b) those in which the criteria for salvation seem to be repentance and faith in Christ, as explicitly required in the apostolic preaching in the book of Acts.

TO DO

How do you react to these comments? Burnaby's position may seem to turn 'the judgement' itself into a further opportunity for salvation *beyond* death. This may be compatible with 'what we know of Christ', but does such a theology leave enough room for the *fear* of judgement, which in the past was such a motivating feature in Christian preaching? On the other hand, does it need to?

When are we to be judged? Although the New Testament refers to judgement primarily in the context of the *parousia*, there are other references that seem to suggest an individual judgement immediately after death (cf. Luke 16.19–31; Philippians 1.23; Hebrews 9.27). If there are two judgements separated by the delay of the *parousia*, the final ('general') judgement begins to seem redundant, as a decision for heaven or hell has already been made – although entering their final state is delayed for all but the perfect.

Which brings us to heaven and hell; and, historically, it is with regard to hell that most theological ink and anxious tears have flowed. The term represents the opposite of heaven, and heaven is a state rather than narrowly a place. Heaven would presumably be physical for embodied resurrected persons (in a new creation or a different universe, but still in time and space); but it could be either a physical or an entirely spiritual/mental reality if it were to 'house' only disembodied souls.

Whatever it is like, *heaven* is in essence a state of unending communion with God. But it is also pictured as a social, and not as an isolated, individual existence. We see this in the communal metaphors that are applied to it in the New Testament, where it is symbolized by a marriage feast, a choir and a city (New Jerusalem – with strong walls and guards but open gates, and without a temple, in Revelation 21). (Many Christians seem to take this imagery far less literally than they do the equivalent symbolic language about hell – for some reason.)

> Whatever these images promise, they suggest more than timeless individual encounter with God, as blessed as that may be. When people speculate, as I have often heard, that they will be able to meet loved ones and talk with them, that they may meet other people . . . and converse with them, that they may meet God and continuously get to know God better, it fits these more social images. These do not convey a static life of doing one thing, even if it is singing in praise. Rather, they suggest a fulfilment of life, not a diminution. (Stiver, 2009, p. 476)

So *hell* must be the opposite of that. It is the result of a willed resistance to and isolation from God's grace, and from our neighbours' cares and needs. 'It is the hellish weariness and boredom of a life lived focused entirely on itself' (Migliore, 2004, p. 347). John-Paul Sartre's famous line, in his play *No Exit*, declared that 'hell is other people'. Whatever he meant by it (probably that the other is often a distorting mirror that reflects us badly, causing suffering), the slogan has caught on. But the spiritual truth is precisely the opposite. Hell's suffering derives from the absence of others, as well as of The Other.

The *dual outcome* of a hell and a heaven seems to be taught in the Gospels (e.g. Matthew 7.13–14; 13.30; 25.46; Mark 9.42–48; Luke 13.1–5; John 3.36).[1] Although Paul also appears to hold to this view, his words sometimes hint at a more universal hope of salvation (e.g. Philippians 2.10–11; Colossians 1.19–20). The medieval imagery of everlasting torture, however, is a misreading of the metaphors of 'unquenchable fire' and 'undying worms' mentioned in the New Testament (e.g. Mark 9.44, 48). These terms read more like vivid symbols of a continuing scene of an ending, a destruction or even a purification – rather than as references to some unending punishment. And some theologians (*annihilationists*), propose that the eternally unrepentant will simply cease to be, which represents a form of 'conditional mortality'.

> What happens to the man who refuses the gift [of eternal life]? . . . He is lost; he ceases to be. This must not be regarded as a pleasant alternative to the pains of punishment in hell. To cease to be is the final tragedy which can befall a living soul who is able to receive the gift of eternal life. Compared with this, punishment which leads to eventual restoration would be infinitely preferable. But of such remedial punishment there appears to be no sign in the words of our Lord. [Though] the idea of annihilation is only dimly perceived in that teaching, there are grounds for saying that such an idea can be inferred from our Lord's words on Hades and Gehenna. (Strawson, 1959, p. 155)

---

1 Although many of Jesus' warnings of disasters may refer to the *historical* situation that was likely to befall Israel, and which did so when the Romans retaliated in response to the Jewish rebellions of the years 66–73 and 117–138.

Others (*universalists*) are even more radical in their rejection of the idea of hell, arguing that their hope that all humankind will ultimately be saved, including the most rebellious, represents the only situation that is compatible with an all-loving God who is in charge of all things. For them, hell is fatal to theodicy and would never be tolerated by God.

> Christ, in Origen's old words, remains on the Cross so long as one sinner remains in hell. That is not speculation: it is a statement grounded in the very necessity of God's nature. In a universe of love there can be no heaven which tolerates a chamber of horrors, no hell for any which does not at the same time make it hell for God. He cannot endure that, for *that* would be the final mockery of his nature. And he will not. (Robinson, 1968, p. 133)

But what of the standard response to these eschatological claims, that 'all that are in Hell, chose it. Without that self-choice there could be no Hell'? Doesn't *God* simply say to *them* 'in the end, "*Thy* will be done"' (Lewis, 1972, pp. 66–7)?

Universal salvation cannot happen by God ignoring or overriding people's own, free rejection of God's person and desire, or of the needs of others. There is no point to free will if we are to lose it when it matters most. Universal salvation can only result from God's patience, which may permit further opportunities after death for repentance, a more radical purgatorial or purifying spiritual development, or continued journeying in the vale(s) of soul-making. This last possibility is advocated by John Hick, who posits 'many [embodied – thus resurrected or reborn] lives in many worlds' before all can achieve their maximum spiritual state of character, transcending themselves in love and entering 'the common Vision of God' (Hick, 1976, Chs 20, 22).

The denial of hell will appeal to those who contend that human punishments can only be justified as a deterrent, a protection for others against further wrongdoing or the reformation of the wrongdoer, and not as a retributive punishment suffered simply to restore the moral balance (cf. pp. 121–2, 123, 127–8). God, they may say, is not worse than we are. Nonetheless, no one holds that salvation for all can be *proved* from Scripture or by theological logic.

> Here I face one of the most irresolvable problems of theology. I must admit that I cannot affirm universalism as a *logical necessity* of Christian faith. On the basis of the ideas of creatural freedom and the limits of God's power, . . . I must grant that everlasting separation from God must be taught as a logical possibility. Instead, the fulfilment of God's will is *a hope and a promise* based upon the love and power of God as revealed in Jesus Christ. If God is the God incarnate in Christ, the God of pure unbounded love, whose love is everlastingly faithful, and whose power is the power of the new creation, then we have all the grounds we need to affirm our hope and confidence that in the end that love and power will draw all creatures to God in God's own time and place. (Inbody, 2005, p. 330)

TO DO

In mythological language, hell exists, but is empty. It is 'there' awaiting any who may be finally lost to God; but in the end none are to be finally lost. Thus the language of the double destiny is existentially valid, truly expressing the momentous character of our moral choices as we face them in the concrete moments of life; and yet it is also subject to qualification in the light of the final sovereignty of God. (Hick, 1973, p. 72)

How would you evaluate such universalism, not only biblically and theologically but also spiritually and morally? In what ways do these topics *matter* to you?

The vision of God

The Bible contains a number of references to the hope of seeing God clearly, perhaps seeing 'God's face' (cf. 1 Corinthians 13.12; 1 John

3.2; Revelation 22.3–4). Later Christian tradition speculated on a full, 'face to face' vision that would be possible in heaven. This vision has even been interpreted as seeing into the essence of God's glory. Some have suggested that the supreme good of this 'beatific [making blessed] vision' has already been allowed to certain favoured persons in their earthly life, such as Moses and Paul. But how can we 'see' *God*, even with 'the eyes of the soul'? What might this metaphor mean? Is it a non-sensory intuition? It cannot involve an absorption into God if we remain separate enough to experience God.

However we interpret it, many will desire *something* along such lines – something that would finally fulfil our longing for God and resolve our fears and doubts at the end of our journey. The metaphors of 'sight' and 'face' are extremely powerful for most of us, with their overtones of intimate knowledge through personal relationships – the situations we find so fulfilling within our present lives. It is no wonder that the Aaronic blessing, which God revealed to Moses for the blessing of the Israelites, remains so moving today:

The LORD bless you and keep you;
The LORD make his face to shine upon you, and be gracious to you;
The LORD lift up his countenance upon you, and give you peace.
(Numbers 6.24–26)

Augustine, although he admits that much in heaven is 'quite beyond my power of imagination', concludes his massive *City of God* with this fervent depiction of the end. It may be too static – or too 'restful' – an image for some, taking a step too far beyond the bustle of the New Jerusalem. Perhaps it represents *the* End beyond that end. But pastoral experience shows that at some point in their life, or in their dying, this is what many people long for. Can something like this form part of the great mystery that lies in our – and God's – Beyond?

After this present age God will rest, as it were, on the seventh day, and he will cause us, who are the seventh day, to find our rest in him . . . The seventh will be our Sabbath, whose end will not be an evening, but the Lord's Day, an eight day, as it were, which is to last for ever, a day consecrated by the resurrection of Christ, foreshadowing the eternal rest not only of the spirit but of the body also. There we shall be still and see; we shall see and we shall love; we shall love and we shall praise. Behold what will be, in the end, without end! For what is our end but to reach the kingdom which has no end? (*City of God*, Book 22, Ch. 30, pp. 1088, 1091)

Further reading

Astley, J., 2010, *SCM Studyguide to Christian Doctrine*, London: SCM Press, Ch. 10.

Hebblethwaite, B., 1984, *The Christian Hope*, Basingstoke: Marshall, Morgan & Scott.

Lewis, C. S., 1972, *The Great Divorce: A Dream*, Glasgow: Collins.

McGrath, A. E., 2007, *Christian Theology: An Introduction*, Oxford: Blackwell, Ch. 18.

Wright, N. T., 2007, *Surprised by Hope*, London: SPCK.

References

Adams, M. M. and Adams, R. M. (eds), 1990, *The Problem of Evil*, Oxford: Oxford University Press.

Astley, J., 2004, *Exploring God-talk: Using Language in Religion*, London: Darton, Longman & Todd.

Astley, J., 2007, *Christ of the Everyday*, London: SPCK.

Astley, J., 2009, 'Evolution and Evil: The Difference Darwinism Makes in Theology and Spirituality', in S. C. Barton and D. Wilkinson (eds), *Reading Genesis after Darwin*, Oxford: Oxford University Press, pp. 163–80.

Astley, J., 2010, *SCM Studyguide to Christian Doctrine*, London: SCM Press.

Astley, J., 2014, *Studying God: Doing Theology*, London: SCM Press.

Astley, J. (ed.), 2000, *Learning in the Way: Research and Reflection on Adult Christian Education*, Leominster: Gracewing.

Astley, J. and Christie, A., 2007, *Taking Ordinary Theology Seriously*, Cambridge: Grove Books.

Augustine, 1972, *City of God*, trans. M. Bettenson, London: Penguin.

Aulén, G., 1970, *Christus Victor: An Historical Study of the Three Main Types of the Idea of the Atonement*, London: SPCK.

Barth, K., 1956, *Church Dogmatics*, IV/1, Edinburgh: T. & T. Clark.

Barth, K., 1966, *Dogmatics in Outline*, London: SCM Press.

Borg, M. J., 2006, *Jesus: Uncovering the Life, Teachings, and Relevance of a Religious Revolutionary*, New York: HarperCollins.

Borg, M. J., 2011, *Speaking Christian: Recovering the Lost Meaning of Christian Words*, London: SPCK.

Borg, M. J. and Crossan, J. D., 2008, *The Last Week: What the Gospels Really Teach about Jesus's Final Days in Jerusalem*, London: SPCK.

Bowden, J., 1983, 'Jesus', in A. Richardson and J. Bowden (eds), *A New Dictionary of Christian Theology*, London: SCM Press, pp. 306–12.

Brunner, E., 1952, *The Christian Doctrine of Creation and Redemption*, London: Lutterworth.

Burnaby, J., 1959, *The Belief of Christendom: A Commentary on the Nicene Creed*, London: SPCK.

Caird, G. B., 1980, *The Language and Imagery of the Bible*, London: Duckworth.

Caird, G. B. with Hurst, L. D., 1994, *New Testament Theology*, Oxford: Clarendon Press.

Catholic Church, 2000, *Catechism of the Catholic Church*, London: Burns & Oates.

Clark, F., 1978, *The Christian Way*, Milton Keynes: The Open University.

Cottingham, J., 2007, 'What Difference Does it Make? The Nature and Significance of Theistic Belief', in J. Cottingham (ed.), *The Meaning of Theism*, Oxford: Blackwell, pp. 19–38.

Cranfield, C. E. B., 2004, *The Apostles' Creed: A Faith to Live By*, London: Continuum.

Cullmann, O., 1958, *Immortality of the Soul or Resurrection of the Dead?*, London: Epworth.

Cullmann, O., 1963, *The Christology of the New Testament*, London: SCM Press.

Cunningham, D. S., 1998, *These Three are One: The Practice of Trinitarian Theology*, Oxford: Blackwell.

Dawkins, R., 1998, *Unweaving the Rainbow: Science, Delusion and the Appetite for Wonder*, London: Allen Lane.

Doctrine Commission of the Church of England, 2005, *Contemporary Doctrine Classics*, London: Church House Publishing.

Dulles, A., 2002, *Models of the Church*, expanded edn, New York: Doubleday.

Dunn, J. D. G., 1975, *Jesus and the Spirit: A Study of the Religious and Charismatic Experience of Jesus and the First Christians as Reflected in the New Testament*, London: SCM Press.

Dunn, J. D. G., 1989, *Christology in the Making: A New Testament Inquiry into the Origins of the Doctrine of the Incarnation*, London: SCM Press.

Dunn, J. D. G., 1992, *Jesus' Call to Discipleship*, Cambridge: Cambridge University Press.

Evans, C. A., 2012, *Matthew*, Cambridge: Cambridge University Press.

Evans, C. F., 2008, *Saint Luke*, London: SCM Press.

Farrer, A., 1966, *Love Almighty and Ills Unlimited*, London: Collins.

Francis, Pope, 2013, *The Joy of the Gospel: Apostolic Exhortation on the Proclamation of the Gospel in Today's World* (*Evangelii Gaudium*), Dublin: Veritas.

France, R. T., 2007, *The Gospel of Matthew*, Grand Rapids, MI: Eerdmans.

Gunton, C. E., 2002, *The Christian Faith: An Introduction to Christian Doctrine*, Oxford: Blackwell.

Gutiérrez, G., 1983, *The Power of the Poor in History*, Maryknoll, NY: Orbis.

Hart, T., 1997, 'Redemption and Fall', in C. Gunton (ed.), *The Cambridge Companion to Christian Doctrine*, Cambridge: Cambridge University Press, pp. 189–206.

Hick, J., 1973, *God and the Universe of Faiths: Essays in the Philosophy of Religion*, London: Macmillan.

Hick, J., 1976, *Death and Eternal Life*, London: Collins.

Hick, J., 1985, *Evil and the God of Love*, London: Macmillan.

Hick, J., 1993, *The Metaphor of God Incarnate*, London: SCM Press.

Hick, J., 1995, *The Rainbow of Faiths: Critical Dialogues on Religious Pluralism*, London: SCM Press.

Hick, J., 2004, *An Interpretation of Religion: Human Responses to the Transcendent*, Basingstoke: Macmillan.

Higton, M., 2008, *SCM Core Text: Christian Doctrine*, London: SCM Press.

Inbody, T., 2005, *The Faith of the Christian Church: An Introduction to Theology*, Grand Rapids, MI: Eerdmans.

Johnson, L. T., 2010, *The Writings of the New Testament: An Interpretation*, London: SCM Press.

Küng, H., 1971, *The Church*, London: Search Press.

Küng, H., 1977, *On Being a Christian*, London: Collins.

Küng, H., 1993, *Credo: The Apostles' Creed Explained for Today*, London: SCM Press.

Lampe, G. W. H., 1963, 'The Bible Since the Rise of Critical Study', in D. E. Nineham (ed.), *The Church's Use of the Bible: Past and Present*, London: SPCK, pp. 125–44.

Lampe, G. W. H., 1966, 'The Atonement: Law and Love', in A. R. Vidler (ed.), *Soundings: Essays Concerning Christian Understanding*, Cambridge: Cambridge University Press, pp. 173–91.

Lampe, G. W. H., 1977, *God as Spirit*, London: SCM Press.

Lane, T., 2013, *Exploring Christian Doctrine*, London: SPCK.

Lewis, C. S., 1972, *The Great Divorce: A Dream*, Glasgow: Collins.

Lloyd, M., 2012, *Café Theology: Exploring Love, the Universe and Everything*, London: St Paul's Theological Centre.

Loughlin, G., 1991, 'Squares and Circles: John Hick and the Doctrine of the Incarnation', in H. Hewitt, Jr. (ed.), *Problems in the Philosophy of Religion: Critical Studies of the Work of John Hick*, New York: St Martin's Press, pp. 181–205.

Macquarrie, J., 1977, *Principles of Christian Theology*, London: SCM Press.

Manson, T. W., 1963, *The Teaching of Jesus: Studies of its Form and Content*, Cambridge: Cambridge University Press.

Markham, I. S., 2008, *Understanding Christian Doctrine*, Oxford: Blackwell.

McCabe, H., OP, 1987, *God Matters*, London: Mowbray.

McGrath, A. E., 2007, *Christian Theology: An Introduction*, Oxford: Blackwell.

McGrath, A. E., 2008, *Theology: The Basics*, Oxford: Blackwell.

McIntosh, M. A., 2008, *Divine Teaching: An Introduction to Christian Theology*, Oxford: Blackwell.

Migliore, D. L., 2004, *Faith Seeking Understanding: An Introduction to Christian Theology*, Grand Rapids, MI: Eerdmans.

Moltmann, J., 1977, *The Church in the Power of the Holy Spirit: A Contribution to Messianic Ecclesiology*, London: SCM Press.

Moltmann, J., 1985, *God in Creation: An Ecological Doctrine of Creation*, London: SCM Press.

Norris, R. A., 1979, *Understanding the Faith of the Church*, New York: Seabury Press.

Okholm, D. L. and Phillips, T. R. (eds), 1996, *Four Views on Salvation in a Pluralistic World*, Grand Rapids, MI: Zondervan.

Pannenberg, W., 1972, *The Apostles' Creed in the Light of Today's Questions*, London: SCM Press.

Price, H. H., 1965, 'Survival and the Idea of "Another World"', in J. R. Smythies (ed.), *Brain and Mind*, London: Routledge & Kegan Paul, pp. 1–33.

Ramsey, A. M., 1936, *The Gospel and the Catholic Church*, London: Longmans.

Ramsey, A. M., 1969, *God, Christ and the World: A Study in Contemporary Theology*, London: SCM Press.

Ramsey, I. T., 1965, *Christian Discourse: Some Logical Explorations*, London: Oxford University Press.

Robinson, J. A. T., 1968, *In the End God*, Glasgow: Collins.

Robinson, J. A. T., 1973, *The Human Face of God*, London: SCM Press.

Schleiermacher, F., 1958, *On Religion: Speeches to its Cultured Despisers*, New York: Harper & Row.

Selby, P., 1991, *BeLonging: Challenge to a Tribal Church*, London: SPCK.

Simpson, J. G. and Lampe, G. W. H., 1963, 'Holy Spirit', in F. C. Grant and H. H. Rowley (eds), *Dictionary of the Bible*, Edinburgh: T. & T. Clark, pp. 389–94.

Smart, N., 1979, *The Phenomenon of Christianity*, London: Collins.

Sölle, D., 1990, *Thinking about God: An Introduction to Theology*, London: SCM Press.

Stiver, D. R., 2009, *Life Together in the Way of Jesus Christ: An Introduction to Christian Theology*, Waco, TX: Baylor University Press.

Strawson, W., 1959, *Jesus and the Future Life: A Study of the Synoptic Gospels*, London: Epworth Press.

Tilley, T. W., 2008, *The Disciples' Jesus: Christology as Reconciling Practice*, Maryknoll, NY: Orbis.

Tillich, P., 1962, *The Shaking of the Foundations*, London: Penguin.

Walton, R. L., 2013, 'Ordinary Discipleship', in J. Astley and L. J. Francis (eds), *Exploring Ordinary Theology: Everyday Christian Believing and the Church*, Farnham: Ashgate, pp. 179–188.

Ward, K., 1990, *Divine Action*, London: Collins.

Ward, K., 2008, *The Big Questions in Science and Religion*, West Conshohocken, PA: Templeton Press.

Watson, D. F., 2010, 'Christology', in C. A. Evans (ed.), *The Routledge Encyclopedia of the Historical Jesus*, Abingdon: Routledge, pp. 107–114.

White, V., 2002, *Identity*, London: SCM Press.

Wiles, M., 1999, *Reason to Believe*, London: SCM Press.

Williams, R., 2007, *Tokens of Trust: An Introduction to Christian Belief*, Norwich: Canterbury Press.

Wink, W., 1998, *The Powers That Be: Theology for a New Millennium*, New York: Doubleday.

Wright, N. T., 2006, *Evil and the Justice of God*, London: SPCK.

Wright, N. T., 2007, *Surprised by Hope*, London: SPCK.

Wright, N. T., 2009, *Justification: God's Plan and Paul's Vision*, London: SPCK.

Young, F. M., 2002, *The Making of the Creeds*, London: SPCK.

Zizioulas, J. D., 2008, *Lectures in Christian Dogmatics*, ed. D. Knight, London: Continuum.